# FINLAND
# IN THE
# NEW EUROPE

# THE WASHINGTON PAPERS

... intended to meet the need for an authoritative, yet prompt, public appraisal of the major developments in world affairs.

**President, CSIS:** David M. Abshire

**Series Editor:** Walter Laqueur

**Director of Studies:** Erik R. Peterson

**Director of Publications:** James R. Dunton

**Managing Editor:** Donna R. Spitler

## MANUSCRIPT SUBMISSION

*The Washington Papers* and Praeger Publishers welcome inquiries concerning manuscript submissions. Please include with your inquiry a curriculum vitae, synopsis, table of contents, and estimated manuscript length. Manuscript length must fall between 30,000 and 45,000 words. All submissions will be peer reviewed. Submissions to *The Washington Papers* should be sent to *The Washington Papers*; The Center for Strategic and International Studies; 1800 K Street NW; Suite 400; Washington, DC 20006. Book proposals should be sent to Praeger Publishers; 88 Post Road West; P.O. Box 5007; Westport, CT 06881-5007.

THE WASHINGTON PAPERS/175

# FINLAND
# IN THE
# NEW EUROPE

## Max Jakobson

Foreword by George Kennan

Published with the Center for Strategic
and International Studies, Washington, D.C.

PRAEGER

Westport, Connecticut
London

**Library of Congress Cataloging-in-Publication Data**

Jakobson, Max.
    Finland in the new Europe / Max Jakobson.
        p.    cm. — (The Washington papers : 175)
    Includes bibliographical references and index.
    ISBN 0-275-96372-1 (alk. paper). — ISBN 0-275-96371-3 (pbk. :
alk. paper)
    1. Finland—History—20th century.   2. Finland—Foreign relations—
Europe.   3. Finland—Foreign relations—Soviet Union.   4. Europe—
Foreign relations—Finland.   5. Soviet Union—Foreign relations—
Finland.   I. Title.   II. Series.
DL1066.5.J35    1998
948.9703'4—dc21        98-21290

*The Washington Papers* are written under the auspices of the Center for Strategic and International Studies (CSIS) and published with CSIS by Praeger Publishers. CSIS, as a public policy research institution, does not take specific policy positions. Accordingly, all views, positions, and conclusions expressed in the volumes of this series should be understood to be solely those of the authors.

British Library Cataloguing in Publication Data is available.

Library of Congress Catalog Card Number: 98-21290
ISBN: 0-275-96372-1 (cloth)
        0-275-96371-3 (paper)

First published in 1998

Praeger Publishers, 88 Post Road West, Westport, CT 06881
An imprint of Greenwood Publishing Group, Inc.

Printed in the United States of America

The paper used in this book complies with the Permanent Paper Standard issued by the National Information Standards Organization (Z39.48-1984).

10   9   8   7   6   5   4   3

For Marilyn

# Contents

# Foreword

Finland, to whose external relationships in the 80-odd years of its formal independence this book is devoted, is a relatively small country. Its population is roughly that of the state of Massachusetts—about 5 million people. To the extent that its inhabitants are known outside their immediate international neighborhood, they are held everywhere in high respect as a strong and tough people, great soldiers in the defense of their own country, and great athletes. They are widely known for their distinguished contributions to world culture, particularly in the fields of architecture and musical composition.

But when it comes to a more intimate association with other peoples, limitations impose themselves. Finland is in a number of important respects a very distinctive country, set off from others by peculiarities in its experience, situation, and consciousness. For this there are a number of reasons. One is geographic location. The country is tucked away in the extreme northeastern corner of non-Russian Europe, with few immediate neighbors, the borders with these latter running in considerable part through desolate semi-arctic regions. Its language resembles nothing spoken anywhere else except in its small cousin-state of Estonia. In many of its outer aspects it would appear to be a Scandinavian country, and indeed in some respects it really is; but here, too, there are significant differences. For all these reasons Finland may be said to have remained a relatively inconspicuous object on the horizons of international life.

Against this background it could be assumed that Finland's

historical experience and present aspect have little to teach us that would throw light on the problems we others have to face at this time. But as the contents of this book will show, the assumption is unwarranted. Precisely because Finland's life continues to be played out on a smaller, more remote, and simpler historical stage, its problems stand out, when perceived from our distance, with a vividness and starkness often obscured when the same problems emerge among all the confusion and cacophony of our own complicated lives.

Roughly the first half of this book is historical. Special emphasis is laid, quite naturally, on the dramatic ups and downs of Finland's situation and involvements in the period of World War II: on the coping with the pressures brought to bear upon it by the great contenders for victory and power in Eastern Europe, Hitler's Germany and Stalin's Soviet Russia; on the two Finnish-Soviet military conflicts to which those pressures led; and on the severe difficulties of the immediate postwar period.

There could of course have been no one better qualified to portray and to appraise this bewildering string of events than the author of this book. Himself an experienced diplomat (Finland's permanent representative at the United Nations from 1965 to 1972), ambassador to Sweden (Finland's most important diplomatic post) from 1972 to 1975, and a leading historian of the Winter War, Max Jakobson has unique qualifications for the understanding and literary treatment of these events; and those qualifications reveal themselves in the authority and the lucidity of his accounts of them.

The final chapters of the book, however, relate to Finland's efforts to come to terms with the fast-moving and perplexing developments of this *fin de siècle* period. These latter have posed many challenges for Finland. How, for example, was a deep-seated and traditional policy of neutrality to be reconciled with the movement toward European unity and membership in any of the individual international associations—NATO, the European Union, the Economic and Monetary Union, et cetera—in which this movement presented itself? To join any of these organizations could of course be seen as a means of associating others in Finland's security problems, particularly in the relationship with the great neighboring power, Russia, which, all recent changes notwithstanding, many Finns continued to view with anxiety. Yet would not that very association imply an impairment of the complete neutrality to which those very same Finns have traditionally been, and remain today, passionately attached?

And how about the much-discussed "global economy"? If major Finnish concerns were to enter successfully into this vast and open-ended competition, would not their growing financial and commercial strength come to overweigh and dominate the modest domestic substance of Finland's economy and threaten the independence of the government itself?

It is, as will readily be seen, not for Finland alone that questions of this nature are now posing problems. For this reason, Mr. Jakobson's authoritative and lucid portrayal of Finland's position should make interesting and useful reading for many others concerned to find the right answers to the peculiar problems of this post-Cold War age.

George Kennan
April 1998

# Preface

This book grew out of an article I wrote in 1996 for CSIS's journal, *The Washington Quarterly*. It was published in the fall issue of that year under the title "Finland: A Nation That Dwells Alone." Several friends, Americans and Finns, urged me to expand the article into a book that would fill the void in up-to-date information on Finland in post-Cold War Europe available in English. What I have now written is not a scholarly and comprehensive work, but rather my personal view, based in part on my own experience, of the century-long struggle of the Finnish people to maintain their independence and their way of life. Having wrested sovereignty out of the ruins of the Czarist empire, Finland defended itself successfully in World War II, preserved its democratic system intact in the ideological contest that followed, and has now finally secured for itself a place in the European Union.

But the story does not end here. Finland now has to deal with the contradictions between the commitment to "ever closer union" and the enduring vitality of nationalism, and with the unsettling consequences of globalization. Finland's security, too, must be seen in a wider context. While NATO moves eastward, the problems of the security of the Baltic region are still unresolved. Thus a book about Finland today is a book about the central issues facing Europe as a whole. And it is bound to be in large part a book about Russia, the unknown factor in the European equation.

I am grateful to the Foundation for Economic Education in Finland for its support. I also thank my former colleague from the Finnish Foreign Service, Mr. Paavo Keisalo, for helping me to get my facts right, and Ms. Sirkka Rytkönen for her diligence and patience in preparing the manuscript through many changes to its final form.

Max Jakobson
Helsinki
May 1998

# Introduction

With less than two years to go, balance sheets of the twentieth century are being drawn up. For Europe the verdict is bound to be harsh. Almost all European nations are haunted by nightmares of humiliating defeats or loss of power and status; few can look back without shame and guilt. It will be hard to find happy exceptions. Switzerland is an obvious choice, except that its reputation has been tarnished by revelations of its dealings with Nazi Germany. Sweden, too, has become a less attractive candidate since its vaunted "middle way" has led to a dead end. But who would come to think of Finland—a country "much admired, often pitied, never envied"?[1] Not many among the Finns themselves, who cultivate a self-image of a nation forever battling implacable Fate. And of course Finland too has its nightmares, notably fratricide in 1918. Yet I believe the record will show that Finland has emerged a winner from the ordeals of the twentieth century.

By joining the European Union (EU) in 1995, Finland has finally moved out of Moscow's shadow. Its position in the international community is no longer defined in terms of the ups and downs of its relationship to its eastern neighbor—that is, as oppressed by, liberated from, or victimized by Russia, nor as a showcase of Finnish-Russian coexistence. Finland now is judged on its own terms—by its economic performance and the quality of its political life.

The Finnish economy has taken great strides during the past century. Technology has all but wiped out the handicaps formerly imposed by the cruel conditions in the northern periphery of inhab-

1

ited Europe. Finland now ranks high among the wealthy nations, with a gross national product per capita on par with that of Britain or Italy and just above Sweden. According to the United Nations "human development index," which takes into account life expectancy, educational standards, and other qualitative aspects as well as gross domestic product, Finland ranks third in Europe and sixth in the world, after Canada, the United States, Japan, the Netherlands, and Norway. And, most important, Finland is one of the very few European states that Eric Hobsbawm lists in his history of the twentieth century as having "adequately democratic political institutions that have functioned without a break" from the end of World War I until this day. Finland has made it "only just," Hobsbawm adds, but then "only just" is good enough in an "age of extremes," which is his description of this terrible century.[2]

Yet Finland remains an unknown country. In the past 50 years, Finland has surfaced only rarely above the horizon of international politics. I once asked former president Jimmy Carter how many times in his four years in office he had had to deal with a matter relating to Finland. After some thought he could recall one such occasion, but could not remember what it was about. His national security adviser Zbigniew Brzezinski makes no mention of Finland in his memoirs. In Henry Kissinger's two-volume account, totaling 2,800 pages, of his eight years at the center of policymaking, Finland appears once—as the place where President Ford met Soviet leader Brezhnev in 1975. In the memoirs of the principal political actors during the Reagan and Bush presidencies, Finland figures only as a stopover on the road to Moscow.

Finns should not complain. The agenda of urgent issues confronting the U.S. president and his advisers is the sick list of the international community: only countries in trouble make it. The absence of any mention of Finland is proof of the success of its policy of minding its own business and keeping out of the way of the big powers.

But there has been a price to pay. Those who make policy and influence opinion in the major capitals have had no incentive to follow Finnish developments; their knowledge of Finland remains superficial and fragmentary. During the Cold War, Finland was at the mercy of the itinerant columnist who after lunch or cocktails in Helsinki was ready to pronounce upon the fate of the Finnish people. Obsessed with Finland's relations with the Soviet Union, visitors from the West almost invariably produced a one-dimensional view of the country, reflecting the prevailing state of East-West relations. In 1939–1940, the Finns were idolized for their fight against the Red Army; in 1941, ostracized for continuing to fight the Russians; in 1945, castigated for refusing to trust Uncle Joe Stalin; in 1948, written off as lost for signing a treaty with Moscow; and finally, in the 1970s, subjected to a form of collective character assassination by the use of the term "Finlandization" to denote supine submission to Soviet domination.

With the collapse of the Soviet empire, the Western view of Finland has of course changed. A reversal of roles has taken place on the international scene. It used to be the Soviets who claimed that their system represented the final stage of the evolution of human societies, while the West rejected the notion that there was a single truth in politics. Now the West believes that its formula of success has universal validity: democracy plus market economy equals political stability and economic prosperity.[3]

Ironically, this too reflects a basically Marxist worldview. It recalls Karl Marx's prediction that the capitalist system, by developing global markets, would force all nations to use the same methods of production and thus "create a world of its own image." Now the market is expected to transform all of Europe, including Russia, in the Western image. All European states follow the same script on their way to greater unity, and each step is rated in terms of its impact on progress toward that goal. Reality is measured against the platonic idea of a Europe united on the basis of common values.

Such is the view from the political summit where government leaders meet to survey the scene. But a descent to the plains and valleys of Europe reveals a different landscape. Just as Marx and his followers failed to grasp the strength of national, cultural, and religious differences, so also the universalist doctrines of today tend to gloss over the stubborn facts that divide the European peoples. The integrating forces of technology and economic interest encounter strong resistance from communities based on historical, linguistic, or ethnic bonds; the ideology of unity clashes with the immutable facts of climate and geography and the peculiarities of national character and tradition.

The Finnish case illuminates the interplay between the universal and the particular. Finland is "one of us"—a democracy and a market economy, now a member of the EU; yet it is also "a nation that dwells alone," as Hungary was described in the days of the

Habsburg empire, set apart by language and historical experience and determined to retain its distinct character.

Ask a Finn to explain this, and he is likely to begin by reminding you that Finland is, after all, a small nation: a phrase pregnant with hidden meaning. It is sometimes said with pride: Look how much we have achieved although we are a small nation. Or it may be said defensively, by way of an alibi: You cannot expect too much from us; we are only a small nation.

Sometimes, however, modesty is replaced by a smug tone of moral superiority, as if there were a special virtue attached to being a small nation; an assumption that once goaded Molotov, Stalin's foreign minister, to respond to a presentation by the Finnish ambassador with the remark: "The fact that Finland is a small nation doesn't mean that you are always right."

This did not sound so amusing at the time as it does today. Molotov spoke more bluntly to the foreign minister of Lithuania in 1940: "You must be realistic enough to understand that the time of small nations has passed." These words spelled the end of the independence of the Baltic states. But they also revealed more generally the essence of what it meant to be a small nation. As defined by the Czech writer Milan Kundera, "The small nation is one whose very existence can be put in question at any moment: a small nation can disappear and it knows it."[4] The first business of a small nation is survival, as Poles remind themselves each time they sing the opening line of their national anthem: "Poland has not yet perished. . . . "

Twice in my lifetime Finland has been written off as lost by the West: first in the Winter War of 1939–1940, when the Finns were left alone to face the Red Army, and again at the end of World War II, when Finland was assigned to the Soviet sphere of influence. Yet contrary to conventional wisdom, Finland survived, emerging from World War II as the only country among Russia's European neighbors not conquered by Soviet forces.

Why Finland succeeded where others failed has mystified the West. During the Cold War, the Finnish case looked like an odd piece left over after the jigsaw puzzle had been assembled. Isaac Deutscher suggested in his celebrated biography of Stalin that the Soviet leader had treated Finland "leniently," because it was a country where he met Lenin for the first time.[5] The explanation tells us more about the intellectual climate prevailing in the Western world at the time than about Stalin's policy. It was taken for granted that had the Soviet leaders wanted to take over Finland they could have done so. Yet a pawn had beaten a rook: it had to be a sacrifice, a move designed to confuse and deceive the West.

When, in October 1961, I went to Washington to prepare for a visit of the Finnish president to the United States, I was questioned by President John F. Kennedy on various aspects of Finnish policy, but what he really wanted to know was something about Soviet policy. "What puzzles us Americans," he said, "is why the Soviet Union has allowed Finland to retain its independence?" That the Finns themselves might have had something to do with maintaining their independence had not occurred to him.

Kennedy's question revealed the conventional view of international relations as the playing field of the interests and aspirations of the major powers. Smaller nations are treated as objects of policy, statistical units in categories of states classified in terms of their relationship to their respective protectors or oppressors, as ours and theirs—pawns to be gained or lost in conflicts or deals between the great. Yet Finland's survival illustrated, not for the first time in history, that in a conflict between a big power with world-wide interests and commitments and a small nation with the single objective of survival, the balance of power cannot be calculated by simple arithmetic. History is made at the margin.

In the winter of 1940 and again in the summer of 1944, Finnish resistance to the Soviet offensives was strong enough to raise the cost of breaking it to a point at which continuing the war against Finland put more important Soviet interests at risk. In 1940, the risk was involvement in a conflict with the Western powers; in 1944, the divisions that had bogged down in Finland were needed for the race to Berlin. In both instances, Stalin decided to cut his losses and make peace with Finland, leaving the Finnish army intact. Finland had to cede roughly one tenth of its territory, but did not suffer the humiliation of unconditional surrender. Apart from Britain, Finland was the only European country involved in World War II that was not occupied by foreign forces, neither by Germany nor by the Soviet Union.

The Finnish people fought when they had to, but stopped fighting in time and adjusted their policy to the realities of power that had emerged as a result of World War II. As the chief ideologue of Finnish nineteenth-century nationalism, J.W. Snellman, a disciple of Georg W.F. Hegel, has written, "Only primitive tribes fight till the last man; a civilized nation must bend to external necessity in order to preserve itself for future generations."[6]

The will of the Finnish people to defend themselves against the Soviet onslaught, as well as their resilience in bending without breaking during the Cold War, had a common source—the vitality of their democratic system. Finland's Parliament has functioned virtually unchanged since 1906, and the constitution as a whole since 1919. Finnish democracy was strong enough to withstand the Fascist virus in the 1930s and to reject the influence of Nazism from 1941 to 1944, at a time when Finland fought on Germany's side against the Soviet Union. And it was strong enough to resist Communist subversion during the Cold War, while Finland pursued a policy designed to placate the Soviet leaders.

Yes, Finland survived World War II, and Finland survived the Cold War. But will Finland survive the European Union—survive, that is, as an independent nation with its distinct identity?

In the three Nordic countries, the issue of national independence was at the heart of the debate on whether to join the European Union. I do not mean that it was a contest between good Europeans and reactionary nationalists. Both sides were nationalists—or, should I say, patriots. The difference between them was that supporters of EU membership were optimists who believe that their country can best further its national interests by joining the Union, while opponents were pessimists who fear that membership is bound to lead to a loss of independence and national identity.

In the end, the outcome of the 1994 referendums in the three countries was determined less by attitudes toward the EU than by geopolitical factors. Norway has NATO, and Sweden has Finland, but Finland faces a land border of 800 miles with Russia. And Finns did not need Professor Samuel Huntington to tell them that this was not simply a border between two states: for centuries it was the dividing line between Western and Eastern Christianity and for 75 years the frontier between Western democracy and the Soviet system; today it marks the greatest welfare disparity in Europe. So the Norwegians believed they could afford to say no to the EU, and the Swedes were almost evenly divided, with only a narrow majority favoring membership, while the Finns voted, 57 to 43 percent, to join. Opinion surveys clearly indicate that many Finns voted yes because they believed the country would be safer inside the Union. Membership, they thought, would finally end half a century of ambiguity by making it clear that Finland was part of the West. Norwegians and Swedes could take that for granted.

By joining the Economic and Monetary Union (EMU) in the first group, Finland leapfrogged over Sweden and Denmark to cement its place in the inner sanctum of the European Union. Although a common European defense remains a distant possibility, the single currency, the euro, scheduled to be adopted in 2002, will serve as a bond stronger than any solemn treaties. Finns need no longer fear isolation in a crisis—for the first time in this century.

But change rolls on. As a by-product of the Balkan war, NATO now occupies center stage in Europe. By taking in three Central European states and at the same time setting up the Joint Council with Russia, NATO has taken the lead in building a post-Cold War security order in Europe. For Finland, as well as for Sweden, this is both reassuring and disturbing. The Baltic region is half in and half out. NATO's door remains open to the three Baltic states, but how long will they have to wait and how can Russia be persuaded to drop its opposition to their entry into the Western alliance? Could accession to the EU satisfy the craving of the Baltic peoples for a secure place in the Western fold? While these questions are debated, Finland too wants to keep its foot in NATO's door.

Russia will of course always be vitally important for Finland. The relationship between Finns and Russians is complex and not all enmity and war. The French historian Fernand Braudel goes so far as to claim that the people known as the great Russians were originally formed by a mixture of Slavs and Finns, with the latter making up the bulk of the population: "barbaric but robust."[7] This view is refuted by scholars today: an analysis of Finnish genes points to a predominantly Baltic-German origin. But obviously through the centuries, intermingling with Russians has taken place. Not surprisingly, Finns are supposed to know better than other Europeans what goes on in the Russian mind. Unfortunately, Finnish leaders have not always been able to anticipate Russian actions.

Today, Finland is free of the constraints imposed upon it as a consequence of World War II. Relations with Russia can be described by the favorite Russian term as businesslike. But Finns are less inclined than other Europeans to judge Russia by its progress, or lack of it, toward the goal of creating a democratic system and market economy. They tend to put more emphasis on the enduring influence of the Russian tradition. In this they may be guided by an instinct for self-preservation: to be always prepared for the worse.

The Russian question is not, however, uppermost in the minds of the Finnish people. It is subsumed under the more general sense of uncertainty about the future that pervades Europe today. Unemployment, taxation, and the erosion of the welfare state are undermining the system of "social democratic capitalism" built up after World War II. Governments are no longer able to control the economy by exclusively national means, yet the European Union lacks the power to take collective action. Thus Europe lives uneasily in a no-man's-land between the two systems: the old one no longer functions effectively, but a new system has yet to be put in place.

The relevance of the nation-state as the basic unit of the international system has been brought into question by the technology-driven globalization of economic activities. If the state withers away, what happens to the nation? The logic of integration points one direction, but political reality another. Nationalism is alive and well, in Finland as elsewhere. This is dismissed by some scholars as a rearguard action that may delay but cannot stop the advance of transnational forces. The Finnish case suggests, however, that the answer could be different.

# 1

# Nationalism

In a public opinion survey conducted in the beginning of 1996, a representative sample of Finns were asked to choose from a number of qualities the ones they believed to be characteristic of the Finnish people as a whole. More than 80 percent placed patriotism, a strong sense of national identity, and the will to defend the country at the top of the list. The Finns are, in a word, a nationalistic people, and proud of it.

When I mention this to friends in Western Europe, they tend to react as if I had told them that the Finnish people are still afflicted by the kind of diseases that have been eradicated in civilized countries. It was different during the Cold War. Nationalism was then a capital crime in the Soviet Union, while the West applauded every manifestation of national independence within Moscow's orbit. Now the West sees in nationalism "a specter haunting Europe." According to one political analyst, "few issues pose a greater threat to the post-Cold War international order than those emanating from nationalism and the quest for self-determination."[1] This is the conventional wisdom of the day.

Those who talk of the "specter" of nationalism do not, of course, refer to American or French nationalism with their universalist pretensions, or to British nationalism so stridently expressed in confrontations between the United Kingdom and the European Union. The specter is the nationalism of lesser peoples whose aspirations threaten the status quo.

Because nationalism is a claim by a people to be recognized as a unique entity, separate from others, it defies scholarly definition, except on a high level of abstraction. In the current debate it is used indiscriminately—for instance, to describe Russian political tendencies that should properly be called imperialist. Political interest, not principle, defines the issue. A noble stand against tyranny in one part of the world becomes an atavistic impulse in another. Palestinian nationalism is encouraged, while the Kurds' claim to independence meets with embarrassed silence. Fighters for Basque autonomy are condemned as terrorists; Welsh and Scottish nationalism is dismissed as quixotic. In the case of the Balkans, more than a thousand years of history is compressed into the single word of nationalism to explain the behavior of Serbs, Croats, or Bosnian Muslims, from which only a short step leads to the belief that all nationalists behave like Serbs, Croats, or Bosnian Muslims. No one mentions the nonviolent, democratic struggle of the Baltic peoples for independence from Soviet rule as an example of nationalism.

Citizens of long-established, powerful nation-states can afford the hypocrisy of deprecating nationalist passions, while at the same time protesting against the subjugation of peoples by foreign invaders or alien rulers. Yet, in practice, stability is almost invariably defended against a nationalist challenge. Boutros Boutros Ghali, former secretary-general of the United Nations (UN), expressed a widely held view when he pointed out that if every claim to independence were to be recognized, the world would become ungovernable. It would create pandemonium, as U.S. senator Daniel Patrick Moynihan has written.[2] Similar opinions have been heard each time an empire has fallen apart, releasing its subject nations to claim self-determination. In 1918, the Finnish people, too, were told by members of older states that their country was too immature to manage on its own. When former Soviet leader Mikhail Gorbachev visited Finland in 1989, he argued that the Baltic countries were far too small to form viable states. When reminded that Finland, a country not much larger than the Baltic ones, had done quite well after seceding from Russia, Gorbachev politely changed the subject, but clearly remained unconvinced.

It is the old story: those who have arrived would like to close the door behind them. But who is to decide, and by what criteria, which nations deserve independence? The question was discussed in the UN Security Council in 1970, at a time when I represented Finland on that body. The idea was to find a way to stop the influx of mini-states into the UN. The U.S. delegate suggested that no state with a population of fewer than 1 million should be considered eligible. This provoked me to make what I believe must be the shortest speech ever made in the United Nations. I said, "Goodbye Iceland!" That put an end to the search for quantitative criteria of national independence, for who would question the reality of the independence of Iceland, a nation of 250,000 people?

"Every nation a state, only one state for the entire nation"—this was the ideal as defined by Giuseppe Mazzini, the prophet of nineteenth-century European nationalism. Finland today is one of the very few nation states that comes close to this ideal. But this was not achieved by conscious design: it is the product of a historical evolution.

The first essential step was not, as is commonly believed, liberation from Russian rule, but separation from Sweden. This came about as a by-product of the deal struck between Napoleon and Alexander I in 1807, in which the Russian czar undertook to persuade or, if necessary, compel Sweden to join Napoleon's blockade against Britain. In the process Russian forces occupied Finland, and the country was annexed to the Russian empire as a Grand Duchy of the czar. Its borders were not drawn up along ethnic or linguistic principles; dialects of Finnish were spoken on both the Swedish and the Russian side of the Grand Duchy. It was, in essence, a geopolitical entity, a buffer state for the protection of St. Petersburg, the Russian capital.

The image of the meeting between the two emperors at Tilsit is engraved upon the collective memory of the Finnish people, just as is that of Molotov and Ribbentrop, the foreign ministers of the Soviet Union and Nazi Germany, meeting in Moscow in August 1939 to carve up Eastern Europe into spheres of influence: two vivid lessons in geopolitics as the primary force that moves nations. Still today, it is a goal of Finland's foreign policy to make sure that the country will not be used once again as small change in a deal between the leaders of the big powers. A sense of geopolitics seems to have been written into the genetic code of the Finnish people.

For Sweden the loss of Finland meant the end of empire, perceived by contemporaries as a humiliating defeat, but in historical perspective a blessing in disguise and the beginning of a spectacular success story. Only once after the Finnish campaign was Sweden involved in war, even then outside its own territory: in the anti-Napoleon coalition in 1814. From then on the Swedish people have enjoyed unbroken peace—184 years by 1998. Finland as a buffer has protected Sweden as well as Russia. Although the other European nations tore each other to pieces in wars, Sweden built up a new kind of empire—an industry with world-wide markets. This in turn provided the wealth that enabled Sweden to finance the social experiment publicized in 1936 by the American journalist Marquis Childs as the "middle way" between callous capitalism and totalitarian communism.

The other party in the forced divorce also fared well. As part of the kingdom of Sweden, Finland had been a poor and neglected area, a "developing region" we would call it today, with no political or cultural identity of its own. The language of education and administration was Swedish; for a Finn the only road to advancement was by assimilation into Swedish culture. Had Finland remained part of Sweden, the Finnish-speaking population, whatever would be left of it, might today be one of the many frustrated linguistic minorities that angrily clamor for recognition.

Having nonetheless fought valiantly against the Russian invaders, the Finnish people found that the switch of allegiance they were forced to accept was rewarded with an enhanced political status, while at the same time they were able to retain the invaluable assets they had acquired during 700 years of Swedish rule: the Lutheran religion, constitutional monarchy, Swedish civil and criminal law, the freedom of the peasantry—in other words, their Western heritage. In terms of geopolitics Finland became part of the Russian empire; in cultural terms Finland remained part of the West.

Alexander I was at the time still influenced by the liberal ideas of the Enlightenment. He was also anxious to gain the loyalty of his new Finnish subjects. In spring 1809 he convened the representatives of the four estates (clergy, nobility, burghers, and peasants) confirming their rights and privileges. The Grand Duchy of Finland was to have its own central administration headed by a Senate and, in principle, its own Diet with its four estates. This meant in effect the birth of a separate Finnish state. As grand duke of Finland, the Russian czar, an autocrat with absolute power in the rest of his empire, accepted the role of a constitutional monarch. Finland, Alexander declared, was thus "elevated as a nation to the ranks of nations."

The meaning of the word *nation* must be understood in the context of the time. Many nations dwelled in the vast house of the Russian czar: Finland was to be one of them. But for the Finns, Alexander's promise to respect the Finnish constitution became a sacred compact between the sovereign and the people and the basis of Finnish self-rule. This did not make Finland a nation in the modern sense of the term. But Finland did acquire in 1809 a territorial identity and an independent administrative structure—a state in search of a nation. Thus Finnish nationalism as it developed during the latter half of the nineteenth century flowed into a ready-made mold. The romanticism characteristic of nationalist movements in Europe was tempered by the mundane tasks of administration.

Finland was at the time a relatively egalitarian society. There were no vast estates, no serfs. The typical Finnish nobleman of the early nineteenth century was a former officer of the Swedish army who farmed a modest-sized estate. The nobility had a long-established tradition of public service. Many educated Finns were drawn to St. Petersburg, a great European center open to talent from every part of the empire. The imperial army in particular attracted young Finns, many of whom attained the rank of general or admiral—among them Carl Gustav Mannerheim, who was later to play a leading role in the attainment and defense of Finnish independence.

A sense of nationhood developed slowly. A nation must have a cultural identity: a consciousness of a shared past and a common destiny. Such a consciousness can only be created by historians and poets, artists, and composers. Without its cultural fingerprints, political autonomy remains an empty shell, as can be seen in so many "instant states" created since the end of World War II.

An emerging nation tends to define itself by exclusion. In the cultural sense, Lutheran Finland with its Western values had no difficulty in marking its separateness from orthodox Russia living under autocratic rule. In the West, however, the line was blurred. The continued dominance of the Swedish language kept Finland culturally linked with the old motherland. The issue of language thus acquired a central significance in the development of the Finnish nation. "Has a nation anything more precious than the language of his fathers?" asked German philosopher Johann Gottfried von Herder, the prophet of European cultural nationalism. "In it dwells its entire world of tradition, history, religion, principles of existence, its whole heart and soul."

The publication in 1835 of the *Kalevala*, one of the great epics of mankind, infused the Finnish people with pride in their cultural heritage; it also made the Finnish claim to nationhood widely known in the civilized world. The drive to develop Finnish, spoken by the majority, into a modern language became the centerpiece of Finnish nationalism. Finally, in the 1860s Finnish was by law granted equal status with Swedish as an official language. This was due to the efforts of members of the ruling elite who, in the spirit of the time, abandoned Swedish and adopted Finnish, a language unrelated to the Indo-European languages. (It belongs to the Finno-Ugrian group of languages represented in Europe by Estonian and Hungarian.) In a collective act of linguistic conversion, many changed their family names from Swedish to Finnish. "We are no longer Swedes, we do not want to become Russians, so let us be Finns": this was the simple credo of the founding fathers of Finnish nationalism. It echoed the slogan of Italian nationalists in the 1860s: "We have made Italy—now we must make Italians."

"Linguistic patriotism," as articulated by Herder more than 200 years ago, is still very much alive. This seems to be difficult for English-speakers to understand. In a comment on the Quebec referendum in 1995, an American columnist expressed astonishment that Canada "should self-destruct over an issue as relatively trivial as language."[3] Far from trivial, language has been through the ages a powerful political force—a tool of oppression as well as liberation. The ancient myth of the Tower of Babel, where the Lord "confounded" the single language and scattered the people throughout the earth, remains a relevant metaphor. The Soviet leaders played god in Central Asia in the 1920s and early 1930s by artificially dividing the common Turkic language spoken by the people into separate "national" languages and imposing the Cyrillic alphabet as a barrier to communication with Turkey. Today, in former Yugoslavia, strenuous efforts are being made to split the Serbo-Croatian language into three different tongues corresponding to the political division of the former federation into sovereign states. In several Western countries—Belgium, Spain, Ireland—language continues to be a core issue, as it is in France, where in 1996 a law was passed criminalizing the use of English words in public signs.

The Finnish-Swedish language controversy, intertwined with issues of class, social status, and economic power, remained at the center of politics for close to a century, up to World War II. Today, both languages enjoy official status, and the rights of the Swedish-speaking minority, about 6 percent of the total population, are protected on terms that, by international standards, can be described as generous. Swedish is still being taught as a compulsory subject in all Finnish schools, and Finnish-speakers now acknowl-

edge the importance of Swedish for Finland's ties with the other
Nordic countries.


## A Nation Is Born

The compact between the grand duke and his subjects, as it was
understood by the Finns, meant that so long as Finland served its
primary geopolitical function, the Finnish people would be able to
live by their own rules. The men who ran Finland in the nineteenth
century found that loyalty to the ruler paid off in terms of freedom
of action in internal matters. They kept what today would be called
a low profile, avoiding any challenge to Russian security or prestige.
They learned through practice the subtle art of steering Finnish
autonomy past potential points of conflict with the vital interests
of the empire. They cultivated a conservative social outlook, shield-
ing the Finnish people from the influence of liberal currents of
thought that might disturb the Russian autocracy. "Leave the Finns
alone," Czar Nicholas I is said to have told his ministers at the
time of the Polish uprising in 1830. "It is the only part of my realm
which never has given us any trouble."

The interplay between Polish rebelliousness and Finnish caution continued. At the time of the second Polish uprising in 1863,
the Finnish philosopher and statesman J.W. Snellman warned
his countrymen against siding openly with Poland against Russia.
Such foolish gestures, he said, would only hurt Finland without
any benefit to the Poles. Finnish loyalty was promptly rewarded.
Alexander II made Finland a showcase for his liberal ideas. During
his reign, Finnish self-government took a great leap forward. His
statue still stands in the central square of Helsinki.

The Diet of the four estates was convened regularly from the
early 1860s onward, thus replacing bureaucratic rule with the begin-
nings of a civic society. The Grand Duchy also established its own
central bank, the Bank of Finland, which introduced its own currency, the markka, in 1860, released it from the ruble five years
later, and tied it to the gold standard in 1878. Industries based
on the country's forest resources were being rapidly developed,
railways and canals were built, foreign trade multiplied. Finland
entered the twentieth century as a modern nation with a standard
of living on par with, for instance, the German part of Austria.

The transformation of Finland during the nineteenth century was dramatic. At the time of the separation from Sweden, Finland was poor and backward. Over most of the country, mere subsistence prevailed as a way of life. The wilderness was more extensive than the occupied and cultivated area. The population of about 900,000 was concentrated in the southwestern corner of the country. In the words of national poet J.L. Runeberg, the Finnish people had to "wrest their bread from ice and snow." In the poorest areas, bread was often made from flour mixed with pine bark. In the famine years of 1867–1868, some 100,000 people, 8 percent of the total population, died of starvation or disease.

Finland's rise out of such poverty, achieved without foreign aid, contradicts the widely held view that the leaders of backward and poor peoples must be excused for using dictatorial methods of government, because no other way leads to economic development: democracy is a luxury only wealthy nations can afford. In Finland, the economy developed parallel with a widening of the political process. Industrialization was speeded up by private enterprise and foreign investments. Modernization brought about national unity, social cohesion, and faith in progress—the conditions required for a democratic system.

Finland's progress inevitably widened the gulf between the Grand Duchy and Russia. The Finnish people enjoyed a higher standard of living and greater political freedom than the rest of the empire. The Finnish economy became more closely integrated into the West, while protected by a customs border in the east. On their passports, Finns were described as Finnish nationals and Russian subjects. Finland even had its own army: all officers and men had to be Finnish citizens and, with the exception of the guard battalion, could not be ordered to serve outside their own country.

Toward the end of the nineteenth century, Finland's success aroused growing resentment among the Russian elite. Finland was accused of taking advantage of the security provided by the empire without paying its proper share of the costs. Traces of this attitude have persisted till this day, as can be seen in Aleksandr Solzhenitsyn's works. In a pamphlet entitled *The Russian Question* published in 1994, Solzhenitsyn points out that during the nineteenth century Finland was able to multiply its national product by six or seven times because it could minimize its defense expenditures. He complained that Finns held high offices in the Russian administration and in the armed forces, while Russians were not allowed to be appointed to public office or to buy property in Finland unless they had obtained Finnish citizenship. And "only a few miles from their capital city Russians had to face Finnish customs inspectors, who refused to speak Russian." All this, according to Solzhenitsyn, was evidence of the failure of czarist policy to prevent "Europe" from cheating Russia![4]

It is true that the Finnish authorities closely guarded their country against Russian influences. In 1914, the number of Russians residing in Finland was only 0.4 percent of the total population. Knowledge of the Russian language was limited. Solzhenitsyn has a point when he claims that Finland was enjoying the best of both worlds. Having served for centuries as a battleground between East and West, Finland lived peacefully as part of the Russian empire for more than 100 years, except for a brief encounter with Anglo-French naval raiders during the Crimean War. The carnage of World War I passed Finland by.

Factors more important than envy soured Finnish-Russian relations at the end of the nineteenth century. The Finnish system of constitutional government came under increasing criticism from Russian conservatives determined to defend autocracy at home. What had been a showcase of liberalism under Alexander II turned into a dangerous precedent under Nicholas II. It encouraged separatism in other parts of the empire and demands for constitutional reform in Russia itself. Russian military leaders, obsessed with the German danger, were dismayed to discover on the doorstep of St. Petersburg a part of the empire that had developed into a foreign country with close cultural and commercial ties with Germany and Great Britain, as well as with Scandinavia. Both external security and internal stability were perceived to be threatened by Finland's special status.

In 1898, General Nicolai Ivanovich Bobrikov, a hardliner known for his tough actions in other parts of the empire, was appointed governor-general of Finland, with the mission of restricting Finnish autonomy and integrating the Grand Duchy militarily and administratively into the Russian system. As Solzhenitsyn put it, "It is not the purpose of imperial policy to make the subject peoples happy." Yet by keeping the Finns happy, Russia had enjoyed maximum security in the North at minimum cost; by arousing Finnish nationalism, Russia created the enemy it sought to contain.

After almost a century of relative harmony, the relationship between Russia and Finland was transformed into a classical con-

frontation between a great power bent upon safeguarding its imperial interests and a small people fighting for its own way of life.
As Isaiah Berlin has pointed out, "A wounded Volksgeist is like a
bent twig, forced down so severely that when released, it lashes
back with fury. Nationalism is created by wounds inflicted by
stress."[5] Many conflicts attributed to nationalism are in fact caused
by the suppression or denial of the right of a people to run their
own lives. Before Bobrikov appeared on the scene, Finnish nationalism had been a cultural phenomenon, embraced by the elite. His
attempt to curtail Finnish self-rule transformed it into a political
mass movement.

At first the Finnish people refused to believe that their sovereign, the grand duke, would break his solemn pledge to respect
the Finnish constitution: he must have been misled by evil advisers.
More than half a million Finns, almost half the adult population,
signed an address appealing to the emperor, and although he refused to receive it, it served its purpose as an unprecedented demonstration of political mobilization. A mood of defiance, eloquently
expressed in *Finlandia*, the music of Jean Sibelius, spread among
the Finnish people. Artists and writers were in the front line in
defense of what was perceived to be the very essence of Finland's
national identity.

The Western world for the first time became aware of the
Finnish national struggle. The Finnish pavilion at the Paris World
Fair in 1900, designed by Eliel Saarinen, the first in a line of great
Finnish architects, received wide attention. More than a thousand
distinguished European intellectuals including Anatole France,
Florence Nightingale, Henrik Ibsen, and Emile Zola, signed "Pro
Finlandia," an appeal addressed to the czar. "Scarcely a single
famous name is missing," remarked the Russian minister who
brought the appeal to the emperor's attention. But it was of course
dismissed as interference in Russian internal affairs.

The Russian policy of repression was met with a campaign
of civil disobedience. Recalcitrant civil servants and judges were
dismissed, prominent Finnish leaders banished to Siberia or forced
into exile, and many young men emigrated to the United States to
avoid conscription into the Russian army. As Russian pressure
mounted, an agonizing debate went on between the conservatives
who advocated appeasement of Russian power and prestige as the
only means of preserving the essence of Finnish national life and
the liberal constitutionalists who insisted on standing fast on legal

rights regardless of the consequences. There were also the activists who prepared for direct action by sending young men to Germany for military training and the left-wing revolutionaries who made common cause with their Russian comrades in the belief that the overthrow of the czarist regime would bring both national liberation and social reform. It was a debate that has a timeless quality: the arguments used then could be applied today wherever nations face the cruel choice between submitting to superior power and engaging in suicidal resistance.

Except for the assassination of Bobrikov in 1904 by a young Finnish civil servant who immediately killed himself, the struggle was carried on nonviolently. On the Russian side, too, the art of repression did not reach the high standards achieved under the Soviet regime. There were no executions, no mass terror, no concentration camps. When a member of the Mannerheim family was forced into exile, he was given a week to put his affairs in order, which at the time was considered harsh treatment, but it did enable his brother Carl Gustav, then a colonel in the Chevalier Guards in St. Petersburg, to travel to Helsinki to bid his brother farewell before he sailed off to Stockholm—not exactly a hardship post.

Many others were treated more harshly, among them my uncle who was banished to Siberia, but returned after the Bolshevik revolution in good health and full of tales about the interesting people he had met in exile. His case was by no means exceptional. This is not to say that there was no suffering or hardship, nor could those involved console themselves with the thought that greater horrors were still to come. On the whole, however, the Russian regime was still bound by fundamental rules of civilized conduct.

Passive resistance gained time, often the most precious asset for a small nation under pressure. A leading historian and writer Zacharias Topelius advised a hotheaded young friend to be patient and wait until "the colossus in the East" would collapse. Finland was first rescued by Russia's defeat in 1905 in the war against Japan and spreading unrest in Russia herself, which forced the czar to concede to demands for constitutional rule. In Finland, the old Diet of four estates was replaced in 1906 by a single-chamber parliament elected by universal suffrage, making Finland the first European country to grant women the vote. This radical reform profoundly affected Finland's future course. It directed the nationalist current into parliamentary channels. The fight against Russian repression became a fight for parliamentary democracy.

Russian policy lurched from repression to reform, then back again to repression, but finally the colossus did collapse. The overthrow of the czarist regime provided Finland with the opportunity to declare full independence on December 6, 1917. But this was not the happy end of the story of Finland's liberation from foreign rule. Once the external threat receded, the social conflict that had been brewing since the beginning of the century exploded into violent confrontation. Although Lenin had recognized the independence of Finland on the last day of 1917, 40,000 Russian troops remained in Finland, and the Bolsheviks encouraged the Finnish socialists to seize power, hoping that revolution would bring back to Soviet Russia what the czar had lost. The "Red guards" formed by the radical wing of the socialist movement clashed with the "White army" led by General Mannerheim, who had returned to his native Finland after 30 years of service in the imperial army. The war lasted from January until May 1918, killing a total of 30,000 Finns, many of whom were victims of terror practiced by both sides.

The victorious Whites called it a war of liberation, but this is still contested today by those who prefer to describe it as a class conflict or a civil war. Objectively, as Marxists might say, we now know that it did mean liberation, because had the Reds won, Finland would surely have come under Soviet rule. But Finland's secession from the Russian empire must be seen in a wider context. In 1917, Germany had won the war in the east, the German army was in full control of the Baltic region, and a German expeditionary force was sent to Finland in spring 1918 to make sure the Whites would win. The conservative political leaders of Finland looked to Germany for protection against a resurgence of Russian imperialism, a potential threat made all the more frightening by the revolutionary designs of the Bolsheviks. A German prince was elected king of Finland to make sure Germany would remain committed to the defense of its northern ally. In return, Finland was prepared to make far-reaching economic concessions.

Had Germany been able to maintain its dominance in the eastern part of Europe, Finland would have become a German protectorate. But in November 1918 the bottom fell out of this scheme. Suddenly, Finland was on its own. The German king-elect had the good sense to withdraw before setting foot on Finnish soil. A complete about-turn of Finnish policy became necessary. The pro-German political leaders stood aside, and Mannerheim, never a friend of Germany, was sent to London and Paris to mend fences. In the parliamentary elections in the beginning of 1919, the republicans gained a large majority. Only then, in May 1919, did the United States and Britain agree to recognize Finland, and France confirmed the recognition she had withdrawn the previous year. Thus the Finns learned early on that "interference in the internal affairs of states" is a fact of international life.

## Prelude to War

In the major capitals of Europe, the entry of the sovereign republic of Finland into the international community was received with a degree of skepticism. A Finnish diplomat who complained to the editor of the London *Economist* that the paper persisted in printing out-of-date maps showing Finland as part of Russia was told that the *Economist* took a long view of international affairs without letting transient phenomena lead it astray. To people used to a world ruled by the great dynasties, the new states that had emerged from the ruins of World War I seemed artificial creations, not to be taken seriously.

This attitude was caught by Anthony Powell, the British author, in his novel *Venusberg* (1932), in which a lady representing a fictional newly independent small country—presumably Finland—tells a British diplomat: "We are only a little country. A little new country. You must not be surprised if sometimes we do not seem to do things so well as you big countries who have been big countries for so long. You big countries do not know what it is like to be a little country. . . . "[6]

There were grounds for concern about the future of the little country Finland. The tragedy of 1918 had left deep wounds. The Whites and the Reds continued their battle on the political arena. In 1930 the Communist Party, which at the time held 23 seats out of 200 in Parliament, was banned on the grounds that it was an agent of a foreign power. Documents that have come to light since the collapse of the Soviet Union prove the case beyond any reasonable doubt. The tragic irony of the Finnish Communists was that, while branded traitors in their own country, they faced the charge of nationalism in the Soviet Union. Many thousands of the Finnish Communists who had fled to the Soviet Union were executed in

Stalin's purges. Those who were caught in Finland were the lucky ones: they were sent to prison and survived.

As one European country after another fell under totalitarian or authoritarian rule, Finland too was infected by the Fascist virus. Fear of the Soviet Union, a sinister power combining traditional Russian imperialism with the Communist vision of world revolution, undermined confidence in parliamentary democracy. Instead of discussion and compromise, leadership and action were called for in defense of Finland's independence. Social Democrats and Liberals were held to be "soft on communism"—unpatriotic. University students dreamed of bringing about unity of blood and soil by liberating the Finnish-speaking population of Soviet Karelia, an area that had never been part of historical Finland.

And yet, democracy prevailed. Finland was one of the few European countries to resist the wave of antidemocratic forces that engulfed the greater part of the continent in the 1930s. In 1937, a coalition government was formed that for the first time since the civil war included the Social Democratic Party as a partner with the Agrarian Party and a small Liberal Party: an act of reconciliation between the farmers and the workers who had savaged each other in 1918. In the parliamentary elections held two years later, the extreme right-wing movement with Fascist trappings (the Patriotic People's League, or IKL) was reduced to a marginal role, with only 8 seats out of 200. The German minister in Helsinki reported the election results to Berlin with the resigned comment that it was difficult to gain sympathy for Nazi Germany in a country in which 90 percent of the people were democrats. In spite of Finland's strong cultural and economic ties with Germany, support for Nazism was confined to the lunatic fringe.

In today's intellectual climate, this account of political developments in Finland in the 1930s may well be read to mean that Western liberalism had emerged victorious. In fact, liberalism remained a feeble force in Finnish politics. "It leaves us cold," wrote Urho Kekkonen, later president of Finland, who at the time was a leading spokesman for Finnish nationalism. The dominant view was that the interests of the nation must be put before those of the individual. But this was not to be achieved by force. Finnish nationalism had been baptized in the struggle for constitutional government and the rule of law against the autocratic Russian regime, and it remained faithful to these values. National unity had to be achieved, not by authoritarian methods, but by reintegrating the losers of 1918 into the parliamentary system. The conservative Right rejected extremism, while the Social Democratic Party adopted a pragmatic and moderate line. A far-reaching land reform, which created close to 100,000 new farms, helped to gain the loyalty of the rural proletariat of tenant farmers and landless laborers, many of whom had joined the Reds in 1918.

Economic progress smoothed the road to greater national unity. Finland recovered from the great depression sooner than most other European countries. This was achieved by policies that would have pleased Milton Friedman rather than John Maynard Keynes. After the pain caused by strict monetarist measures, living standards rose rapidly in the latter half of the 1930s.

An unexpected bonus was produced by the decision of the Finnish government in the early 1930s to pay back the loan received from the United States immediately after World War I. This was done as part of a general effort to improve Finland's credit rating. Had two or three other European states taken similar action, the Finnish decision would hardly had been noticed. But as it happened, Finland was the only country that paid its debt to the United States, and this turned what had been a routine matter into one of the most successful public relations operations of all time. Soon every schoolboy in the United States knew at least one thing about Finland—the country that paid its debts. Repayments were stretched out to last as long as possible. Even at the height of World War II, when Finland's relations with the United States were at a low point, the Finnish ambassador made his annual call to the U.S. Treasury Department, waving a check for the benefit of press photographers. Finally, at the end of the 1940s, what remained of the loan was converted into a fund to finance scholarships for Finns wishing to study in the United States.

In foreign policy, too, the mid-1930s was a turning point. The League of Nations had lost its credibility, and Hitler's rise to power foreshadowed a reign of force and violence in Europe. The overriding issue for Finland was to find a way to make sure that it would not be drawn into a conflict between Germany and the Soviet Union. The first step was to improve Finland's international image. Moscow considered Finland a German satellite, and a similar view was widely held in Western Europe, even in Sweden. To change this perception, the Finnish government declared in December 1935 that it would adhere to a "Scandinavian orientation": the neutrality of Finland, the government stated, could best be preserved in association with the other Scandinavian nations whose loyalty to the concept of neutrality was universally acknowledged.[7]

From time to time there was even talk of a Scandinavian or Nordic defense alliance, but this was a stillborn idea. The four Nordic states (now five with Iceland) have a great deal in common, but are divided by geopolitical realities. In the 1930s they could not agree on a common enemy: Finns feared Russia, Danes Germany; Swedes could not decide which to fear more; Norwegians believed they were safe from both.

A more realistic concept was put forward by Sweden's foreign minister Rickard Sandler: military cooperation between two or more Nordic countries in limited areas and with limited commitments. The Aaland Islands were an obvious point for such cooperation. In the hands of a great power, as Napoleon once put it, Aaland would have been a "pistol aimed at the heart of Sweden." The islands had been demilitarized by an international convention in 1921, and Swedish military planners were anxious to fill the vacuum. In the course of 1938, a joint Finnish-Swedish plan for the defense of the islands was worked out; in January 1939 it was formally confirmed by the two countries. Because a revision of the convention was necessary, the plan was submitted to the other signatory powers for approval. Significantly, the Swedish government insisted that Soviet consent also be obtained, although the Soviet Union had not signed the convention. But Moscow said no, and in the face of Soviet opposition the Swedish government retreated: Swedish opinion was not prepared to accept a commitment that might involve Sweden in a Finnish-Soviet conflict. Thus the limits of Nordic cooperation were exposed.

In secret talks during 1938 and early 1939, the true nature of Soviet policy was revealed to the Finnish government by Stalin's special emissaries. They explained that it was not enough for Finland to promise to maintain neutrality. Without Soviet help, they argued, Finland would not be capable of defending itself. The Germans would force their way through Finland, and the Red Army was not prepared to remain on the border to wait for the enemy: it would advance as far as possible to meet him. As a Russian statesman had said during the Crimean War, the Russian people could not feel safe unless their soldiers stood guard on both sides of the country's borders. Only a Finnish promise to accept military assistance from the Soviet Union could be regarded as a sufficient guarantee for Soviet security. As for the Aaland Islands, Moscow had no objection to their remilitarization provided the Soviet Union, instead of Sweden, would take part in the project. In addition, Finland was requested to allow the Soviet navy to use four islands in the Gulf of Finland as bases for the defense of Leningrad.

The secret Soviet soundings were rejected by the Finnish government. The goal of Finnish policy was to keep the country out of any future clash between Germany and the Soviet Union, not to switch sides and substitute Soviet for German protection.

At this point it is tempting to speculate: What if? Would a firm stand by Sweden on the Aaland Islands have deterred Stalin from attacking Finland? Would not the projected Finnish-Swedish neutrality pact have served Russia's security interests more effectively than the military bases Moscow sought to acquire? We shall never know. What we do know is that Finnish diplomacy failed to achieve its objectives either in the West or in the East. The Swedes would not engage themselves in the defense of Finland, and Moscow insisted on something more tangible than declarations of neutrality. Mannerheim, then chairman of the Defense Council, concluded that there was no choice but to prepare for war. Ahead of almost everybody in Europe, he predicted that Hitler and Stalin would make a deal, and it would be at the expense of Finland and the other states in between. He urged the government to seek a major loan from the United States to finance purchases of modern weapons. But he was not heeded. Finland at the time was governed by a group of men whose great strength was their rational approach to politics. Thanks to them, Finland had become a prosperous and stable country. But they failed to grasp the strength of the irrational forces unleashed in Europe in the 1930s.

And yet, on another level, the Finnish people were prepared for the existential test that lay ahead. As a schoolboy in Helsinki in the late 1930s, I did not take much interest in politics—very few of us did—but I remember vividly how we all were suffused by the prevailing mood of unquestioning patriotism. Every able-bodied male served two years in the armed forces, and in addition a voluntary organization providing military training had a membership of 130,000, while a sister organization of 105,000 members prepared girls for defense duties. Instinctively, we took it for granted that one day such activities would prove useful.

Rebecca West, the British writer, visited Finland in 1936 and sensed the mood of the people. She decided to write a book on Finland as an example of a small nation ready to defend its freedom against a powerful tyranny. But then she went to Yugoslavia and found a more colorful background. She missed her story by three years.

# 2

# Survival

In the late 1930s, Finland faced a dilemma shared at all times by small nations living in a no-man's-land between two mutually hostile great powers. In theory, the choice was between neutrality and seeking the protection of one side against the other. In practice, however, Finland had no real choice.

It would have been unthinkable for the Finnish people to accept the protection offered by the Soviet Union. Both history and ideology ruled it out. The Finnish government knew what the Soviet leaders meant by protection. This had been spelled out in detail by the Soviet foreign minister Vyacheslav Molotov in his talks with an Anglo-French delegation in May 1939. He had proposed that the three powers should guarantee the security of the states between Germany and the Soviet Union against both direct and indirect aggression. Pressed to explain the term indirect protection, Molotov said that if, say, the Lithuanian government, for whatever reason, under German pressure or on its own accord, were to adopt policies considered by Moscow to be damaging to Soviet security interests, that would be indirect aggression justifying a Soviet intervention.[1] Submitting to Soviet protection under such terms would have been the political equivalent of unconditional surrender: a judgment validated by later events in other countries bordering on Russia.

The alternative of seeking protection from Germany, the ally of 1918, had substantial support in Finland where Nazism was perceived to be the lesser of two evils. But this alternative too was rejected. The fear was that an alliance with Germany might invite a preemptive strike from the Soviet Union.

What remained was neutrality. Implicitly, however, Finnish neutrality in the 1930s rested on assumptions that were never clearly discussed and therefore not widely understood. The unspoken premise was that the ideological antagonism between Nazi Germany and Communist Russia was a permanent condition of life, ensuring a balance of power in the Baltic region. Germany was expected to keep the Soviet Union in check, while in case of a German invasion of the Soviet Union, Finland would be able to stay on the sidelines as it had in World War I. These were the private thoughts of public men; officially, the hope was expressed that peace would prevail.

Yet, as Mannerheim almost alone had understood, peace between Hitler's Germany and Stalin's Russia was the worst alternative, short of total war, for the small states in between. The brief announcement issued in Moscow on August 24, 1939, informing the world of the nonaggression treaty signed between the Soviet Union and Germany—later known by the names of the two foreign ministers as the Molotov-Ribbentrop Pact—shattered the very foundations of the international order that had emerged in the Baltic region as a result of the collapse of the Russian empire. The secret protocol attached to the treaty was not immediately known, but it was easy to guess that Moscow must have obtained from Hitler what it had failed to extract from the Western powers: a free hand in the Baltic area.

In the course of one month, Poland was crushed by the German war machine, and the country was divided as had been agreed between the two dictators. It took a further two weeks for the Soviets to bully the governments of the three Baltic states—Estonia, Latvia, and Lithuania—into accepting "mutual assistance treaties," granting Soviet forces access to all the military bases south of the Gulf of Finland that Russia had lost in World War I. And on October 5 the Finnish government received an invitation—a summons really—to send a delegation to Moscow to discuss "concrete political questions."[2]

Stalin himself explained to the Finnish delegation what these were. He said he needed more depth for the defense of Leningrad, and it could be obtained only at the expense of Finland. The Finnish border had to be moved farther north from the city, and the Soviet navy had to have a base on the southern coast of Finland, at Hanko close to Helsinki.

The Finnish government made a desperate search for support.

But Berlin advised it to be sensible and to give in. Stockholm told the Finnish leaders not to expect military aid from Sweden. London and Paris were uninterested, realizing that the base Stalin wanted could only be used against Germany. Washington was bound by law to remain neutral. The Finnish leaders knew they stood alone, and they agreed to give up some territory north of Leningrad. But they refused to yield the base Stalin asked for, fearing it might be used to subvert Finnish independence. On this issue the talks in Moscow broke down, and at the end of November 1939 Stalin launched his attack. For a hundred winter days the Finns held out, but in the end they had to make peace on terms that were worse than the ones they had rejected before the attack. Stalin got the base he wanted as well as a great deal more territory than he had originally demanded.

This tale was trivial in the context of world history: throughout the ages bloody skirmishes have been fought along the edges of empires. In the vast drama of World War II, the Soviet-Finnish conflict was merely an incident within an episode, a local Soviet campaign to force a recalcitrant pawn into the square assigned to it in the deal between Stalin and Hitler.

Yet the Winter War is remembered, or rather half-remembered like a legend from a distant time, more widely than many larger campaigns that had a more direct bearing on the outcome of the struggle between the great powers. Its emotional impact, at the time, was immense. The Finnish stand against overwhelming odds offered the Western world a cause without blemish: the Finns defended democracy and freedom and justice, all the things the Western democracies believed in but had at the time little chance actually to fight for.

A vast reservoir of frustrated idealism was released into a flood of sympathy for Finland. Volunteers offered themselves from as far away as Abyssinia. Kermit Roosevelt, son of the late president Theodore Roosevelt, announced the formation of an international brigade. In Britain, the roll of volunteer units to be sent to Finland read like extracts from Debrett: anyone who had ever spent a skiing holiday in St. Moritz was qualified. Robert Sherwood was inspired to write his great Broadway success *There Shall Be No Night*. President Franklin Roosevelt spoke of "the rape of Finland," and Winston Churchill called the Soviet invasion "a despicable crime against a noble people." The French government ordered the Soviet trade mission in Paris to be closed; Italy recalled its ambassador from

Moscow. And a message of encouragement from Uruguay was solemnly read in the Finnish Parliament.

The Finnish people, having had no previous experience of being at the center of world attention, were dazzled by the extravagant expressions of sympathy and admiration. Like simple country folk who take the polite phrases of society literally, they were led to believe that practically the entire civilized world was on the point of rushing to their aid. Perhaps this was a useful self-deception; for what Finns in those days needed most was faith and hope, and to sustain them it was necessary to believe that a rescue party was on its way. But afterward the word "sympathy" acquired an ironic twist in the Finnish language.

On another plane, too, the Winter War had an impact far wider than its military limits. Its political repercussions ranged from crisis in German-Italian relations to the fall of the Daladier government in France. It roused the League of Nations from its deathbed to expel the Soviet Union. It brought neutral Sweden to the very edge of war and helped to breach the isolation of the United States. It sent the Allied governments on what Lord Alanbrooke, chief of the Imperial General Staff, later called a wild goose chase for a new front in the North. It inspired French schemes of knocking the Soviet giant off its clay feet. It was an incident that almost unhinged the power alignments in World War II.

The Winter War continues to mystify historians. Yet Stalin's demands were neither original nor unexpected. Already Peter the Great had said that "the ladies of St. Petersburg could not sleep peacefully" so long as Finland remained in enemy hands. Stalin said the same thing in less elegant language. In his talks with the Finnish negotiators, the Soviet leader revealed himself as the supreme traditionalist. His strategic concept could have been lifted straight out of the archives of the Russian Imperial General Staff. It was not only conservative: it was antiquated.

"You ask which power could attack us," Stalin said in the course of the negotiations. "The answer is: Britain or Germany. Once a war between these two is over, the fleet of the victor will sail into the Gulf of Finland. Yudenich [the White Russian general who fought the Bolsheviks in the Civil War in 1919] attacked along the Gulf, and later the British did the same. . . . "[3] Stalin went on to recall that the czars had 12-inch guns on both shores at the mouth of the gulf, and now the Soviet Union had to have the same defense. That was why a naval base at Hanko on the southern coast of Finland was needed.

In explaining his proposal to move the frontier on the Karelian Isthmus, Stalin told the Finnish negotiators that he had asked Ribbentrop why Germany had attacked Poland and had received the reply that the Polish frontier had to be moved farther from Berlin. "Since we cannot move Leningrad," Stalin continued, "we must move the border." The distance from Leningrad to the Finnish border had to be no fewer than 70 kilometers in order to make sure that the city would be out of the reach of modern artillery on the Finnish side.

The Finnish negotiators tried to persuade Stalin that Finland was determined to remain neutral and would resist any foreign attempt to use Finnish territory for an attack against the Soviet Union. Such assurances Stalin brushed aside with the remark: "They will not ask you, they will come anyway." The military officer attached to the Finnish delegation then pointed out that the security of Leningrad was entirely dependent on who held the southern shore of the Gulf of Finland, for the kind of naval assault along the narrow waters of the Gulf that Stalin seemed to fear was simply not feasible under modern conditions. But Stalin dismissed this as pure theory.

The arguments of the Finnish military expert were proved right by events. The Soviet base at Hanko, which was finally acquired at great cost, turned out to be completely useless against Germany. The Germans never attempted to send their navy against Leningrad; they came by land, and once they had overrun Estonia, Hanko was isolated and had to be evacuated. The only direction from which Leningrad remained safe during World War II was that of the Karelian Isthmus, for in spite of German pressure, Finland refrained from joining the German attack on the city in 1941–1944, just as it had refused to take part in the White Russian march on Petrograd in 1919. It was not until 1955, after Stalin's death, that the Soviet leaders tacitly recognized the validity of the Finnish arguments by returning to Finland their naval base. But in October 1939, Stalin was still obsessed with the past. He was pointing his guns at the ghosts of the civil war and the ineffectual British intervention.

Once Stalin had spoken, the Finnish leaders were faced with the full weight of Soviet power and prestige. They conceded that the

Soviet Union had a legitimate concern with regard to the security of Leningrad and were prepared to accept a frontier adjustment north of the city, as well as to lease some of the islands in the Gulf of Finland. But they balked at permitting the Soviet navy to establish a base at Hanko at a distance of 110 kilometers from the Finnish capital. They feared that the base might be used to force Finland to servitude. Even accepting at face value Stalin's assurance that the base was needed solely for the purpose of defending Leningrad against intrusions from other powers, its effect would have been to destroy the credibility of Finnish neutrality.

On this issue, the Finnish-Soviet talks broke, and on November 9, 1939, the Finnish delegation returned to Helsinki. What followed was an interlude that, in the light of after-knowledge, had an air of unreality. Inexplicably, Finland seemed to relax. Some of the reservists who had been mobilized at the beginning of the negotiations were sent on leave, city dwellers who had been evacuated were given free train rides home, schools that had been closed resumed work. The government was confident that the talks could still be resumed and advised the nation to prepare itself for a long period of uncertainty, during which the Finns would have to learn to "plow their fields with a rifle strapped to their back."

This view was supported by most diplomatic observers and "usually well-informed circles," including those in Moscow itself. Military experts, both Finnish and foreign, argued that a winter campaign could not possibly serve Soviet interests. And they were of course quite right. Had the Soviet leaders foreseen in November that by the end of the year half of their European forces would be frozen fast in the Finnish snow, they may well have thought twice about invading Finland. But the experts failed to foresee Stalin's blunder. The Red Army struck on November 30, 1939, at the onset of one of the severest winters of the twentieth century.

The main offensive on the Karelian Isthmus aimed to destroy the fortifications built there and to move on to the capital, Helsinki. The Soviet armies north of Lake Ladoga were ordered to cut Finland into three parts and occupy the Petsamo area on the Arctic Sea. For these tasks the Soviet Union had assigned 26 divisions, one motorized army corps, five armored brigades, heavy artillery, 1,000 airplanes, several ships, and 100 submarines. The total strength was 500,000 men and 2,000 tanks. Against this force Finland was able to deploy 9 divisions, 75 airplanes, a modest naval force, and coastal artillery.

On the day the Soviet offensive launched, it was revealed in Moscow that the Red Army had received its marching orders in response to a request for aid from "the democratic government of Finland," a fictional body composed of Finnish Communists in exile and headed by O. W. Kuusinen, a former leader of the Reds in the Finnish civil war, who had fled to Russia in 1918 and there risen to a prominent position in the Comintern, the organ directing the world Communist movement. Setting up puppet governments had been standard Soviet practice in the various operations carried out in the beginning of the 1920s to recover territories that had been part of the czarist empire but had seceded during the turmoil of the revolution and civil war. Kuusinen's job was to provide a fig leaf to cover what the rest of the world considered naked aggression.

But if the Soviet leaders believed that the Kuusinen government might rally the Finnish workers to the side of the invaders, they had utterly misread the mood of the Finnish people. The civil war of 1918 could no longer be rekindled. Whatever internal differences and doubts had existed were wiped out by the open challenge to Finnish sovereignty. The question whether more concessions ought to have been offered to avoid war became irrelevant: the Soviet Union recognized only the Kuusinen government and rejected all attempts to resume negotiations. The choice was between fighting and unconditional surrender.

The conduct of the initial Soviet operations indicates that Moscow expected an easy march to Helsinki. So did the rest of the world. But Finnish forces, though heavily outnumbered, succeeded in stopping the Soviet advance on the Karelian Isthmus. Along the long eastern border, large columns of invaders were totally annihilated. The Finnish tactic of letting the heavily armed Soviet columns advance along the roads and then cutting them into pieces succeeded brilliantly. By Christmas the entire Soviet offensive had bogged down. Stalin was forced to reassess the situation. At the beginning of January 1940, a complete reorganization of Soviet forces was undertaken and reinforcements were brought in. But Finland too was able to mobilize more men. By early February, 13 Finnish divisions faced 47 Soviet divisions.

The British and French governments also did some rethinking. At first they had been reluctant to get involved in a struggle that seemed doomed to fail. But the initial success of Finland's defense changed their minds. The Allied governments were under pressure from public opinion to do something to save Finland. A northern expedition was judged not only to be a popular move but also to offer a chance to hit at Germany from a new direction. On their way to Finland, the Allied forces could take over control of the Norwegian coast and occupy Sweden's iron ore mines. With such goals in mind, the Supreme War Council decided in the beginning of February 1940 to send an expeditionary force to Scandinavia, provided Finland appealed for aid.

In retrospect, the Allied plan was almost farcically inept. The troops assigned to the northern adventure were pitifully inadequate. They could not have saved Finland. Nor is it likely that Hitler would have stood idly by while the Allies occupied northern Norway and Sweden. The whole of Scandinavia would have been plunged into war, with disastrous consequences all round.

Yet the Allied plan did help Finland—so long as it was not carried out. It induced the Soviet government to reconsider its Finnish policy. Stalin's declared purpose was to keep the Soviet Union out of the war between Germany and the West. The success of this policy was endangered by the Finnish campaign, which threatened to involve Soviet forces in a clash with the Allies. In the beginning of February 1940, the Soviet government let it be known through Stockholm that it was prepared to resume negotiations with the Finnish government. Kuusinen was no longer mentioned. For Finland, this was a momentous victory. From then on, the war was no longer about Finland's independence; it was about territory—a negotiable issue.

But Soviet prestige was now in need of repair. The peace terms were far in excess of Stalin's original demands. In addition to the base in Hanko and the islands in the Gulf of Finland, Finland was asked to cede the entire province of Viipuri up to what had been the frontier of Peter the Great: once again Stalin explicitly invoked this historical precedent. To back up this demand, Soviet forces in February began a new offensive on the Karelian Isthmus that was far more powerful and more skillfully led than the one in December; the Finnish defense line on the road to Viipuri was soon broken.

Throughout February and during the first week of March, the Finnish government was torn between the uncertainties of Allied aid and the awful prospect of peace on Soviet terms. London and Paris kept pressing the Finns to appeal for aid. Never before in history had two great powers so insistently urged a small nation fighting for its life to accept their rescue mission. The Allied troops were already waiting in their ships: all that was needed was a signal from Helsinki. Yet in the end the Finnish government decided to reject the offer of aid and make peace on terms that meant ceding to the enemy more territory than had previously been given up by the army.

That it was a wise decision cannot be doubted. It was based on the cool appraisal of Marshal Mannerheim and his generals who realized that Allied help would be too late and too little. But it was also an expression of a deep-seated reluctance on the part of the Finnish political leaders to leave the fate of the nation in the hands of the great powers.

## The Second Round

In the West, the spotlight quickly moved to new campaigns, fresh tragedies. Finland once again sank below the news horizon of the international media. Soon enough, *There Shall Be No Night* was again being played to full houses—with Greece as the scene of the action.

For Finland, however, the Winter War was only the first act in the Finnish-Soviet drama. The peace treaty signed in Moscow in March 1940 was supposed to create "precise conditions of reciprocal security" between Finland and the Soviet Union. In fact, the end of fighting was followed by an intense war of nerves. Soviet pressure to prevent closer ties between Finland and Sweden and interference in Finnish domestic politics were taken to mean that Moscow was determined to complete by subversion the task it had failed to carry out by military means. The fate of the Baltic states, which were annexed by the Soviet Union in summer 1940, sharpened Finnish anxieties. That Finland was next on the Soviet list was indeed confirmed in November 1940 when Molotov told Hitler in Berlin that his government intended "to solve the Finnish question" in the manner it had applied to Bessarabia and the Baltic states. But Hitler said no. His generals were already busy planning Operation Barbarossa, the invasion of the Soviet Union, and they intended to make Finland part of it.[4]

The first hint of the change in German policy had been received by the Finnish government in August 1940. Finland was offered the chance to buy arms from Germany in return for allowing German troops to pass through Finland to and from occupied Norway.

Sweden had already agreed to a similar German request, while Finland had just granted the Soviet Union the right of transit to the Hanko base.

At the time, the Finnish-German transit agreement was welcomed by Finnish leaders as a counterweight to Soviet pressure. Their hope was that the restoration of a balance of power between Germany and the Soviet Union would enable Finland to maintain its neutrality. In fact it proved to be the point of no return for Finnish policy. It was the first step in a systematic German campaign to tie Finland to Hitler's war plans. The transit agreement was in reality a cover for the future movement of German troops from Norway, not back to Germany, but through Finland into the Soviet Union. On June 22, 1941, the day the German invasion of the Soviet Union was set in motion, Hitler announced that in the North his troops stood "side by side" with their Finnish comrades-in-arms.

In a formal sense, the Finnish government was still uncommitted, and its first reaction to Hitler's announcement was to declare its neutrality. But this lacked credibility. There had been collusion between the Finnish and German military leaders, and a strong opinion in Finland welcomed the German invasion as an opportunity to recover what had been lost in 1940, or even to create a "greater Finland" including the Finnish-speaking Karelians living under Soviet rule. In any case, with German troops in Lapland poised for attack and Soviet forces in their base in Hanko, neutrality could not have been maintained for long. In fact it lasted four days. On June 25, the Soviet Union launched air attacks against targets on Finnish territory, and in the evening of that day, the Finnish government declared that the country was at war with the Soviet Union.

By joining Hitler's war against the Soviet Union, Finland had acted according to the Machiavellian principle "that for the purpose of saving the country no proposition ought to be rejected . . . the defense of the country is always good no matter whether effected by honorable or ignominious means." Paraphrasing Winston Churchill's famous comment on the German invasion of the Soviet Union—"If Hitler had invaded hell, I would have said something in favor of the devil"—the Finnish leaders were prepared to welcome the devil as their ally against the Soviet Union: the enemy of your enemy is my friend. To a majority of Finns, the Soviet Union and communism were a deadly threat; Nazi Germany a more distant evil. Some of those who remembered World War I hoped that World War II would have a similar end: first Germany would defeat Stalin, then the West would defeat Hitler. But the Finns used a long spoon to sup with the devil. Finnish policy was to insist that Finland was waging a separate war, coinciding with but not part of the German-Soviet struggle. It was called the "Continuation War"—the second round of the conflict that had opened in November 1939. Finland was not an ally of Germany: it was a cobelligerent. Nor was Finland a German satellite: Nazi ideology made no headway in Finland, and German attempts to promote it were firmly rejected. Thus Finland never discriminated against its Jewish citizens.

The conduct of Finnish military operations was designed to underline the separate character of Finland's war. After recapturing the territory lost in 1940, the Finnish troops moved into Soviet Karelia to establish a defensive line along the river Svir connecting Lake Onega with Lake Ladoga. But there they stopped, and German requests for Finnish participation in the offensive against Leningrad or the Murmansk railway were refused.

The finer points of the Finnish case were lost on public opinion, or even on most governments, on either side of World War II. Cobelligerency was a concept too sophisticated to make much impression on nations engaged in a fight for their lives. Germans tended to look upon Finland as an ally; in Western countries, it was regarded as a friend of the enemy. The vast fund of sympathy and admiration for Finland created by the Winter War was largely dissipated. Yet the separate character of the Finnish-Soviet conflict was recognized by the U.S. government, which refrained from declaring war on Finland.

Fred Iklé's book *Every War Must End* contains a banal truth that often puts statesmanship to its severest test.[5] After the German defeat at Stalingrad in January 1943, the Finnish government decided it had to find a way to end the war against the Soviet Union. But how and when? Timing was the crucial issue. To make the move too early would risk German retaliation; to leave it too late would mean going down with Hitler.

Peace feelers put out in the beginning of 1943 provoked German threats of "extreme action." A year later Finnish emissaries went to Moscow to find out the terms on which peace could be concluded, but the Soviet demands were rejected as too harsh. The real reason was that the German forces were still in control of the entire eastern coast of the Baltic Sea, within easy striking distance from Finland, while the Finnish army still stood along the river Svir, deep in Soviet territory. The Finnish leaders hoped to use this "position of strength" to gain a better bargain.

This proved to be an illusion. On June 9, 1944, as the Allies were landing in Normandy, more than 20 Soviet infantry divisions, under cover of one of the most devastating artillery barrages of World War II and backed by more than 400 combat planes, launched an offensive against the Finnish lines on the narrow front of the Karelian Isthmus. They broke through on the western shore along the road to Viipuri; the Finnish forces had to withdraw all along the isthmus, and from Soviet Karelia as well, to avoid encirclement. A Finnish request for peace talks was met with a Soviet demand for surrender. At the same time, Germany offered military assistance on condition that Finland commit itself not to make a separate peace. The choice was between surrender and a fight to the bitter end.

The dilemma was resolved by Finnish president Risto Ryti, who gave the pledge required by the Germans in the form of a personal letter addressed to Hitler. He deliberately exceeded his constitutional powers so as to avoid committing the Finnish government. His personal word was enough for the Germans, who sent both troops and arms to the Karelian Isthmus. The German troops were of little use, but the modern weapons received from Germany were important. By the middle of July, the Soviet offensive was stopped before it had reached the 1940 border. The Finnish army was severely bloodied but still unbeaten.

Once again Finnish resistance succeeded in raising the cost of conquest beyond what the Soviet leaders were prepared to invest on a peripheral front. Soviet military historians have revealed that the objective of the offensive begun in June 1944 was the occupation of southern Finland. But once it had been stopped, Stalin ordered his troops to regroup for defense. He needed his crack divisions more urgently elsewhere—for the race to Berlin.

The time gained by Finland was of decisive value. Germany, hard-pressed on two fronts, could no longer retaliate effectively. In the beginning of August 1944, Risto Ryti resigned and was replaced by Marshal Mannerheim. The new president informed Hitler that he did not regard Ryti's pledge as binding on him. Stalin on his part no longer insisted on surrender: thus Moscow, too, implicitly recognized the separate character of the Finnish war. On

September 19, 1944, an armistice agreement was finally signed in Moscow.

The peace terms restored the frontier of 1940, except in the far north where the Soviet Union annexed Petsamo with its valuable nickel mines and its ice-free port on the Arctic sea. A Soviet naval base was again established on the southern coast of Finland, this time on the peninsula of Porkkala, which is even closer to Helsinki than is Hanko. Finland had to undertake to pay a war indemnity to the Soviet Union in the form of industrial goods and to hand over all former German assets. The Finnish merchant marine had to be placed at the disposal of the Allied powers. Finland also had to drive out the German troops—200,000 men strong—from Lapland, and it took a campaign of six months to force them to withdraw across the Arctic frontier into Norway. On their way they laid waste the entire province of Lapland: this was Hitler's revenge for Finland's treachery, as he called it, in making peace before Germany's final doom.

The entire population of the area ceded to the Soviet Union— more than 400,000 people—chose to leave their homes rather than live under Soviet rule: they had to be resettled. An Allied Control Commission, in which the Soviet element was dominant, was installed in Helsinki to supervise the implementation of the Armistice Agreement. The Communist Party was legalized and was feeding on the misery and suffering caused by three-and-a-half years of fighting. The Western powers, still engaged in the last phase of their struggle against Germany, had no interest in the fate of a small nation that in their view had taken the wrong turn.

Finland had lost the war, it was said. And this is of course true, if the Finnish-Soviet conflict is seen as a traditional war over territory. But to take such a view would be to miss the point. Finland was not conquered. Its social fabric remained intact, and the continuity of its political institutions unbroken. In this fact lies an achievement that transcends the conventional meaning of such terms as defeat or victory. For in the end Finland did not fight for Karelia or Hanko. It fought for national survival. When the fight was over, Finland was a nation crippled and exhausted. But Finland survived. This may seem a pitifully unheroic end to a story of so much effort and sacrifice, suffering, and blood. But for a small nation, in the iron times of World War II, survival was a rare triumph.

The cost was heavy. Finland lost 87,000 men in 1939–1945, or 2.3 percent of the population. Every village has its war memorial. André Malraux, during a visit to Finland as French minister of culture in 1963, was taken to see the war graves in a rural cemetery and told that every soldier killed in action whose body could be found was taken home to be buried. Visibly moved, Malraux exclaimed: "Enfin un peuple civilisé!" A civilized people, not only because they honor those who have sacrificed their lives for the nation's freedom, but also because they had the wisdom to stop fighting in time. In his letter to Hitler, Mannerheim wrote in August 1944:

> Germany will live on, even if fate should deny you victory in your fighting. Nobody can give such an assurance regarding Finland. If this nation of barely four million be defeated militarily, there can be no doubt that it will be driven into exile or exterminated. I cannot expose my people to such a risk.

## Postmortem

Could war had been avoided by a more conciliatory policy in 1939? It was, after all, possible after the end of the war to reconcile the independence of Finland as a Western democracy with the security interests of the Soviet Union in the Baltic area. Could not a similar accommodation have been achieved without bloodshed? Could Finland have stayed neutral in 1941 so as not be tainted by association with Nazi Germany?

The questioning started the moment the guns were silent. The agonizing debate on the rights and wrongs of the wartime policies was less a serious search for the historical truth than a way to come to terms with the new realities of power in the aftermath of World War II. Self-criticism was part of the policy designed to appease the Soviet Union. Later the generational cycle also played its part. The sons of the heroes of the Winter War felt the urge to mock everything their parents had held sacred, including the fight for independence. One more turn of the generational cycle was needed before a balanced national consensus on the war could be reached.

Today, only the few surviving die-hard Communists question the view that Finland had no choice but to fight in 1939. In light of Soviet actions throughout Eastern Europe, the notion that Stalin could have been satisfied with what he had asked for in November 1939 lacks credibility.

Motives and intentions of dictators vary with opportunities and capabilities. Stalin himself said to the Finnish negotiators in November 1939 that his demands represented the minimum necessary to ensure the security of the Soviet Union: "My military advisers would like me to ask much more." Once war had started, the minimum demands were superseded by the maximum objective embodied in the Kuusinen government. In the case of the Baltic states, Stalin also moved from minimum to maximum: in September 1939 he was content with military bases; in July 1940 the three Baltic states were incorporated into the Soviet Union. In view of his repeated references to historical precedents, it is reasonable to assume that it was Stalin's ambition to recover for the Soviet Union all the territories, including Finland, that had been lost by Russia in World War I. In his biography of Stalin, General Dmitri Volkogonov provides circumstantial evidence to support this assumption. He quotes a dispatch of the Soviet envoy in Berlin, dated two days after the German invasion of Poland, in which he reported what Hitler had told him as follows: "As a result of the war, the situation that has existed since the Versailles agreement of 1920 will be liquidated. With this revision, Russia and Germany will reestablish the frontiers as they were before the First World War." According to Volkogonov, Stalin had underlined the last lines in thick red pencil: he had become a participant in the revision.[6]

After the Winter War, Finland was squeezed into a corner between Germany and the Soviet Union. The Red Army was in control of the Baltic area, while Hitler's forces were masters of the European continent as well as of Denmark and Norway. Isolated from its western markets, Finland was economically dependent on Germany. Had the Finnish leaders rejected Berlin's offer of support and insisted on neutrality, the country could not have been saved from war. Hitler would not have respected Finnish neutrality in 1941 any more than he respected Swedish neutrality; he violated the latter by blackmailing the Swedish government into allowing German troops to march from Norway through Sweden into Finland for an attack against the Murmansk railroad. Finland would have been drawn into the conflict not as an autonomous actor, but as a battlefield between Germany and the Soviet Union, finally to be liberated by Soviet forces.

It can now be seen, as if in virtual reality, what submission to Soviet occupation and control would have meant in Estonia, a country closely related to Finland in language and culture. A cheap trip by ferry from Helsinki to Tallinn across 40 nautical miles of water is to traverse 50 years of history. Before World War II, Estonia had a living standard equivalent to Finland's; today, its gross domestic product, or GDP, per capita is one tenth of the Finnish figure. As Estonian president Lennart Meri, a profound thinker and writer, has pointed out, the condition of Estonia after 50 years of Soviet occupation provides Finns with justification for the sacrifices they made in fighting for their freedom.[7]

Meri rejects the widely held view that Estonia had no choice but to submit to the Soviet demands. Obviously, Estonia could not have prevented the Soviet occupation. Its small army would have suffered terrible casualties. But submission did not save the Estonian people from heavy losses: many were deported and vanished in the Gulag, and many others fled to the West. To the physical casualties must be added the moral and mental injuries inflicted by Soviet oppression. In historical perspective, Meri believes, resistance could have had an intrinsic value.

The Hungarian uprising in 1956 is a case in point. It has been described as "the victory of a defeat." Thereafter Soviet leaders treated Hungary with greater circumspection. Timothy Garton Ash has written about the sympathy Hungary has received from people around the world who had hardly known the country existed or had regarded it rather negatively. That sympathy, he points out, remains a national asset as Hungary seeks to join the European Union and NATO. Even more important, the self-respect of the Hungarian people has been immensely strengthened.[8]

On the other side of the hill, total silence reigned for almost 50 years. In the Soviet Union, the war against Finland was known as the "forgotten war." More accurately, it was a war that the Soviet people were instructed to forget: a non-war, described in official texts dismissively as an "armed conflict," as if it were no more than a minor border incident. Yet documents recently unearthed from Defense Ministry archives list Soviet casualties as 130,000 killed, 170,000 wounded, and 65,000 disabled by illnesses. Scholarly works referred to it briefly or not at all. According to an authoritative history of the Soviet Union, "the Finnish militarists, acting on orders of Fascist Germany and reactionary circles of other countries of the West . . . provoked the war between the USSR and Finland."[9]

This was the official line all the way from Stalin through the first years of Mikhail Gorbachev's rule.

A first hint of a break came on the eve of the fiftieth anniversary of the war. In September 1988 I visited Moscow at the invitation of the Novosti Press Agency and had a long discussion on Finnish-Soviet relations with its chief, Valentin Falin, who shortly thereafter was promoted to head the international department of the Communist Party's Central Committee. He had read the German edition of my book on the diplomacy of the Winter War and suggested that I write an article on the subject for publication in a Soviet periodical. He also promised to put me in touch with Soviet historians who, he said, were busy revising the Soviet version of events.

In January 1989 I received word that General Dmitri Volkogonov, director of the Institute of Military History in Moscow, was prepared to discuss with me the origins of the Winter War. Together with two editors of a Finnish weekly magazine, I met Volkogonov and listened to an hour-long monologue that could be compressed into one brief sentence: It was all Stalin's fault. According to Volkogonov, the nonaggression treaty with Germany had been necessary to buy time, but it was wrong to enter into a secret agreement with Hitler on the division of Eastern Europe. Further, Stalin was justified in demanding a frontier adjustment and the naval base in Finland, but it had been a mistake to break off negotiations and take military action. Stalin and Molotov, Volkogonov claimed, had decided on war without even informing the rest of the Politburo. Instead, they should have continued negotiations with Finland. When I asked whether Stalin's ultimate goal had been to conquer Finland and incorporate it into the Soviet Union, Volkogonov feigned to be quite shocked: "That is unthinkable, for Finland's independence had been recognized by Lenin himself, and Stalin was a faithful disciple of Lenin."

This was glasnost Gorbachev-style: not freedom of speech or a genuine search for historical truth, but a selective assortment of revelations designed to serve the political interests of the Gorbachev regime. At the time Stalin was the evil spirit; Lenin was still untouchable. (A few years later Volkogonov was dismissed from his post, after which he published his revisionist biographies of Stalin and Lenin.)

In April 1989 I did receive a request from Falin's agency to write an analysis of the origins of the Winter War, with the promise that it would be published unchanged. In September 1989 it ap-

peared in the monthly magazine *Rodina* (*Motherland*), published by
the Communist Party organ *Pravda*, and provided Soviet readers
with their first chance to find out what had really happened half
a century earlier.

Blaming Stalin was an attempt to evade the real issues raised
by the Winter War. The series of blunders committed by the Soviet
leaders revealed their inability to see the world as it really was.
The closed Soviet system failed to produce reliable information
and analysis of the Finnish situation. The reports of the Soviet
representatives were distorted to fit the ideological bias of their
masters. Moscow was told that the Finnish working class was on
the point of revolt, that the army was plagued by desertions, and
that the government was opposed by powerful left-wing groups.
Even Alexandra Kollontay, then the Soviet minister in Stockholm
and a cultivated person with close personal ties to Finland, recorded
in her private diary fantasies of U.S. and British "imperialist machi-
nations" designed to provoke Finland into war against the Soviet
Union.

By contrast, it is worth recalling a correspondent's perceptive
analysis, published in August 1939, in the Swiss newspaper *Neue
Zürcher Zeitung*. It pointed out that the parliamentary elections held
in July had shown solid support for the government's policy of
Scandinavian neutrality and that any attempt by the Soviet Union
to treat Finland as a Baltic province would meet with determined
resistance. Had Stalin been a reader of *Neue Zürcher Zeitung*, the
Winter War could have been avoided. But he believed his own
men in the field, as well as, presumably, the advice of Kuusinen,
who must have been dreaming of a triumphal return to his native
country.

Nikita Khrushchev has described in his memoirs a meeting at
Stalin's apartment in the Kremlin on the eve of the Finnish war.
The others present were Molotov and Kuusinen. Khrushchev found
Stalin determined to go to war in case Finland rejected the Soviet
demands. But he also firmly believed that war would not be necessary: "All we have to do is to raise our voice, and if they don't
listen, we will fire a shot from a cannon and the Finns will put up
their hands and agree to our demands."[10]

Stalin was a man in a hurry. The pact with Hitler had offered
him a unique opportunity of realizing Russia's historic ambitions
along its western borders, but he could not afford to dawdle.
"Everything in this world can change," he had told the Finnish

negotiators. The war in the west was still in its phony stage; there were rumors and even feelers of peace, and peace in the west would have freed Germany to turn eastward again. Before that happened, Stalin had to reap the full harvest of his German deal. The advance in the Baltic area was only part of it. Equally important, and for many Russians more important, was opening the road into the Balkans. There Bessarabia, the former Russian province lost to Romania, was the first objective, and the capture of Bessarabia was to bring the Soviet forces to the edge of the Romanian oil fields. But Stalin apparently was reluctant to take on Finland and Romania at the same time, and so Bessarabia had to wait while he dealt with the Finns.

Technically, Stalin could claim a belated victory, but in fact, as Khrushchev pointed out, the war against Finland ended in a moral defeat for the Soviet Union. Several of the divisional commanders of the Red Army were court-martialed and shot; Defense Commissar Voroshilov, a civil war hero, was kicked upstairs to a less demanding post; and Kuusinen was banished to the miserable little town of Petrozavodsk as president of the Autonomous Republic of Soviet Karelia. (An agile man, he was brought back to Moscow by Khrushchev, who made him a member of the Politburo before his death in 1964 at the age of 82.) But no heads rolled at the top of the Soviet hierarchy. Stalin personally had been in charge of the war policy from beginning to end: there was no one else to blame. No wonder he wanted people to forget it.

Yet the Winter War set in motion undercurrents that affected the course of World War II. The poor showing of the Red Army on the Finnish front induced Hitler and his generals to believe that they could repeat in the east the lightning strike they had carried out so brilliantly in the west. After the first winter of fighting in the snow and mud of the vast Russian steppes, Hitler unexpectedly arrived at Marshal Mannerheim's headquarters on June 4, 1942, ostensibly to congratulate the Marshal on his seventy-fifth birthday, but in fact to explain what had gone wrong on the eastern front. One banal detail in Hitler's rambling talk summed it all up: The German tanks had not been supplied with antifreeze! The offensive was supposed to have reached its goals before the onset of winter. Later, Hitler's number two, Hermann Göring, went so far as to claim that Stalin had staged the war against Finland in a clever plot to mislead the Germans.

Stalin of course knew otherwise. As soon as the war was over, a postmortem was held at a meeting of the Chief War Council and the Central Committee of the Communist Party. Marshal Voroshilov, then still defense commissar, presented a lengthy report on the lessons of the war with Finland. It opened with a remarkable confession:

> I have to say that neither I, as Defense Commissar, nor the General Staff, nor the Leningrad military district command, had any idea of the peculiarities and difficulties involved in this war. . . . The Finnish army, well organized, armed and trained for local conditions and tasks, turned out to be highly manouverable, staunch in defense and well disciplined.[11]

Voroshilov went on for many pages to describe the inadequacies of Red Army intelligence, poor technical supply, cumbersome communications, and poor winter clothing and food for the troops. Many top commanders were not up to the task, Voroshilov said. But no one referred to the real reason why the Red Army had been led by incompetent officers. The great majority of officers with a higher military education had fallen in Stalin's purges in 1937–1938. According to Volkogonov, all military district commanders had been removed, as well as 90 percent of district chiefs of staff and their deputies, 80 percent of corps and divisional commanders, and 90 percent of staff officers and chiefs of staff.

In his closing speech, Stalin noted that the Finnish war had revealed the backwardness of the Soviet Armed Forces and called for their fundamental restructuring and a sharp increase in size. The experiences of the Finnish war, he said, should serve as a lesson in modern warfare.

Stalin admitted that the Red Army had been poorly prepared for the task, but argued that the timing had been right: Germany was engaged in the west, but for how long? The Soviet Union had to seize the opportunity and strike before it was too late. But he went on to blame the commanders for imagining that the Finnish campaign would be a picnic, like the occupation of eastern Poland.

What Stalin later told Winston Churchill about the Finnish war reveals the mendacity of his dealing with his Western allies. As Churchill has told it, Stalin began talking about the past "in the cordial atmosphere" of dinner at Yalta. The Finnish war, he said, began in the following way:

The Finnish frontier was some twenty kilometers from Leningrad (he often called it Petrograd). The Russians asked the
Finns to move it back thirty kilometers in exchange of territorial
concessions in the north. The Finns refused. Then some Russian
frontier guards were shot at by the Finns and killed. The frontier guard attachment complained to Red Army troops, who
opened fire on the Finns. Moscow was asked for instructions.
These contained the order to return the fire. One thing led to
another and the war was on. The Russians did not want a war
against Finland.

Did Churchill believe all this? His memoirs contain no comment on Stalin's reminiscences.[12]

According to Volkogonov, the principal lesson of the Finnish
war for Stalin was that a war against Germany had to be averted
or at least postponed as long as possible. Stalin feared the Soviet
forces would not be ready to take on the Germans for many years.
His orders were to avoid anything that could provoke Hitler to
break his pact with the Soviet Union. Stalin ignored reports received
from Soviet spies warning him of Hitler's plans to invade the Soviet
Union. According to Marshal Chukov, "all of Stalin's actions and
thoughts on the eve of the war were subordinated to the single
effort to avoid war, and this generated in him a certain belief that
war would not occur." The military leaders were not allowed to
take defensive measures until it was hopelessly late.[13]

Altogether, the Finnish resistance to the Soviet invasion made
a profound impression on Stalin. He respected military prowess
and nothing else, as was shown by his famous question about the
Pope's divisions. He had thought that the Finnish divisions did
not amount to much, but the war changed his mind. During a
discussion on Finland at the Tehran conference in December 1943,
Stalin told Roosevelt and Churchill that "any nation that fought
with such courage for its independence deserved consideration."[14]
After the war he went out of his way on several occasions to pay
tribute to the skill and courage of Finnish soldiers. Finland in his
eyes had passed a crucial test of manhood. This influenced his
attitude for the rest of his life.

Such a Darwinian interpretation of history is no doubt repul-
sive to the rational mind, but that is not sufficient ground for
dismissing it. The way Stalin's mind worked was revealed by his
conversation with Tito in April 1945, as reported by Milovan Djilas.

"This war is not as in the past," Stalin said at one point. "Whoever occupies a territory also imposes on it its social system. Everyone imposes his own system as far as his army can reach."[15] Stalin's words remind me of a remark made by Czar Nicholas I in 1850: "Where the Russian flag has once been hoisted it must not be lowered."

The Russian flag was not hoisted in Finland. Finland remained free. True, the Finns had no more than marginal control over the external circumstances of their country during World War II. Their freedom of choice more often than not was freedom to choose between the bad and the worse. But ultimately it was their own decisions, not decisions imposed by others, that determined their fate. When shooting a rapid one must keep rowing in order to steer, however futile or even absurd that may seem to someone watching from the shore. So too did the Finns keep control over their own affairs, even at times when the current of events seemed irresistible. And they were prudent enough not to attempt to steer upstream, at least not for too long.

# 3

# Neutrality

Eight years after the Berlin wall was pulled down, the nations of Central and Eastern Europe are still haunted by the memory of Yalta, a symbol of deceit and betrayal. The only exception among Russia's European neighbors is Finland. Ask a Finn what Yalta stands for, and he is likely to reply that it is a second-rate holiday resort frequented by people who cannot afford to fly to Southern Europe or the Caribbean. And yet, Finland is the only country where the principles agreed upon by Stalin, Roosevelt, and Churchill at Yalta in February 1945 were actually carried out. The agreement was—as Roosevelt and Churchill understood it—that the Soviet Union was entitled to make sure neighboring countries would be run by "friendly governments" prepared to respect the "legitimate security interests" of the Soviet Union, but that these governments must be freely elected by the peoples themselves. The one country in which such a marriage between the interests of Soviet security and parliamentary democracy was consummated was Finland, where "free and unfettered elections," as prescribed at Yalta, were held in March 1945 within a month of the Big Three Conference, at a time when Hitler was still directing operations from his bunker in Berlin and Finnish troops were driving the Germans out of Lapland: the first elections to be held in war-torn Europe.

The reason why this was possible in Finland was not because it had been so decreed in Yalta. Finland was hardly even mentioned at the conference. "Free and unfettered elections" were prescribed specifically for Poland. But it took almost half a century before such elections could be held in Poland.

Why could not Poland have been more like Finland? After half a century, the question still lingers on, as reflected by Zbigniew Brzezinski in his 1986 book *Game Plan*: "The issue for the Soviet Union is whether to accept eventually a Poland that is more like Finland or to insist on continued ideological-political subordination."[1]

In Moscow's view, the differences between Finland and Poland were profound. Strategically, Finland was peripheral, Poland pivotal. West of Finland was neutral Sweden; west of Poland, Germany. At Yalta, Stalin described Poland as a corridor through which the Germans had attacked Russia twice in 30 years. He insisted the Soviets had to have effective means to keep it closed.

There was, however, another important difference that arose from the political and social conditions of the two countries themselves. The political structure of postwar Finland was not hammered together in a deal between the victorious powers, to be imposed upon the country from the outside. Finland emerged from the war with its political system intact, without an army of occupation on its soil. Free and unfettered elections were an integral part of the Finnish system. The decision to resume the normal electoral process interrupted by the war was made several months before the Yalta Conference. It was not dictated by the Big Three.

Poland presented a sharp contrast. Its social fabric had been torn to shreds by five years of German occupation, and a new political system was constructed under the guns of the Red Army. The attempt made by Churchill and Roosevelt at the Yalta Conference to create a Poland in the image of their own societies was doomed to fail: liberal parliamentary democracy had no roots in Poland.

The same was true of the other countries of Eastern and Central Europe that had been occupied by Soviet forces, with the single exception of Czechoslovakia where free elections were held in May 1946. In all the others, various types of authoritarian regimes had been in power in the period before World War II. None had had much practice with holding free and unfettered elections.

How then was Finland different from Czechoslovakia, a country with a strong democratic tradition that nonetheless was overtaken by the Communists after World War II?

In the first years after the end of the war, political developments in Finland and Czechoslovakia did seem to run along parallel lines.

In both countries the Communist Party gained strong support in the first postwar elections. In Finland, the People's Democratic League, a Communist-led front organization, received 23.5 percent of the votes and 49 seats out of 200 in Parliament. The League, the Social Democrats, and the Agrarian Party, all three being roughly equal in strength, formed a coalition government that, like its counterparts in France and Italy, mirrored the Grand Alliance that had won the war and was expected to run the postwar world.

The election results were taken to mean that the Finnish people had understood the message of Yalta and were prepared to adjust themselves to the new order that was expected to emerge in Europe. But a closer analysis points to a different interpretation. The results reveal that the Finnish political structure had remained remarkably stable. In the last prewar elections in July 1939, the Social Democrats as the only left-wing party—the Communists having been banned—won 89 seats out of 200. In 1945, the combined Left won 99 seats—10 more than before the war, which was not a landslide. Moreover, the leadership of the Social Democratic Party remained staunchly anti-Communist, which meant that there was a solid majority, 151 to 49, in defense of democracy. Few of the people who voted for the People's Democratic League were actually Communists; they simply supported the most radical social reformer.

The Communists could nevertheless claim that they now represented the wave of the future. They demanded a complete reorientation of Finnish policy not only in foreign relations but also in economic and social terms and the removal from public life of those who were responsible for the policy that had led to war. They insisted on putting their own man into the post of minister of the interior, and he used his power to appoint Communists to key positions in the police forces. Many Finns feared their civil liberties were in danger.

At this dark moment of their country's history, the Finnish people turned for leadership to two old men who appeared to personify the past: Marshal Mannerheim (b. 1865), the former czarist officer, who to the end of his days persisted in using the term Bolshevik to describe the Soviet leaders; and the former monarchist Juho Kusti Paasikivi (b. 1870), a retired banker who had been the chairman of the Conservatives—a party then confined to impotent opposition. Both were nineteenth-century men who had grown up in a period when Finland had been able to live at peace as part of the Russian empire. And precisely because they were men of the past, they could reassure the nation that the necessary adjustment to the realities of postwar power could be contained within the established frame of Finnish freedom and democracy.

Mannerheim's unassailable personal authority ensured national unity at the critical moment in September 1944, when the armed forces, still unbeaten in the field, had to withdraw behind the border agreed upon in the armistice talks and turn against their former comrades-in-arms, the Germans in the north. Under his leadership, the transition from war to peace was made without internal disruption. But in April 1946 the 79-year-old Marshal, whose health was failing, retired, and Paasikivi was virtually unanimously elected president for the remainder of Mannerheim's term. In 1950 he was reelected, at the age of 80, for a full term of six years.

Paasikivi brought to his office a lifetime's experience of addressing the problem of reconciling Finnish national aspirations with Russian interests. He had begun his political career in the early years of the century, at a time when the autonomy of Finland was facing the challenge of czarist repression. He had then joined the group of conservative politicians who had been convinced that the essential national interests of the Finnish people, above all their cultural identity, could be preserved only through prudent appeasement of the strategic interests and prestige of the Russian empire. In 1920 he headed the team that negotiated the first peace treaty between independent Finland and the Soviet Union, and he was successful in obtaining Soviet recognition of Finland's historical frontiers: too successful, as he later was to point out, in that these frontiers almost touched the suburbs of Leningrad, thus creating a sense of insecurity in the minds of the Soviet leaders. In October 1939 Paasikivi was chosen to lead the Finnish delegation that had to face Stalin's demands, and after the Winter War he served as Finland's minister to Moscow.

With the approach of the German-Soviet clash, Paasikivi found himself increasingly out of tune with the spirit prevailing in Helsinki, and he resigned a few weeks before Finland once again was embroiled in war with the Soviet Union. He remained an unofficial adviser to the government, but stayed out of office, and so, in 1944, was untainted by association with Nazi Germany. As he later noted, a small nation like Finland always needs not an opposition shadow cabinet, but a reserve team ready to step into office whenever a turn of the great wheel of world politics makes a change of leadership necessary. In 1919, the turn of the wheel had thrown Paasikivi, the pro-German monarchist, out of office; in 1944, it brought him back.

Although the outcome of the war had in effect confirmed Finland's existence as an independent state, the former foundations of its security had been destroyed. The balance of power in Europe had changed, irrevocably it then seemed. Germany was in ruins. The Western powers were allied with the Soviet Union; neither their interests nor their influence extended to the eastern shores of the Baltic. Indeed, U.S. policy at the end of World War II was to warn Finland not to expect any kind of support against the Soviet Union. Finland was alone, exposed to the overwhelming Soviet force. Not surprisingly, the Finnish General Staff, without informing the political leaders, began to store arms into secret caches in preparation for a guerrilla war that seemed inevitable.

To this situation Paasikivi offered a concept of Finnish-Soviet relations that was not only tailored to fit the prevailing strategic realities but also designed to restore the faith of the Finnish people in an independent future. He had always argued that the Russian interest in Finland was primarily strategic and defensive. It was to ensure that the city Peter the Great had built would be safe from an attack through Finland. This, according to Paasikivi, was a "legitimate interest," a subtle phrase in the spirit of Yalta that conveyed both the direction and the limit of his policy of appeasement. It was designed to assure the Soviet government that its need for security would be satisfied, while serving notice that Finland would not yield to demands going beyond the legitimate—ideological demands, for instance. By convincing the Soviet leaders that Finland under no circumstances would turn against them, Paasikivi believed the Finns could secure their own independence and way of life. He thus undertook a double task of persuasion: to make the Kremlin trust an independent Finland, and to make the Finnish people bend themselves to the facts of power and work together to achieve the first objective.[2]

And the Finnish people worked hard, in those first years after the end of the war, to convince the Soviet leaders that Finland could be trusted to keep its word. Fulfillment of the terms of the Armistice Agreement (and later the Peace Treaty of 1947) was given priority over all other tasks. The goods demanded by the Soviet Union as a war indemnity were delivered punctually on schedule. (During the first year, they amounted to 15 percent of Finland's national product; in the second, to 11 percent.) Finland is probably the only country in modern history that has voluntarily paid its war reparations in full.

An even heavier burden for the war-crippled nation was the task of resettling the population of the ceded territory. The peace terms reduced Finland in size by more than one tenth; the prewar population of the ceded areas had been 436,000, or 12 percent of the total. Literally no one had stayed behind the new frontier; the Russians had taken over a land emptied of human life. In the aftermath of World War II, when large-scale ethnic cleansing was carried out by the allied powers, the fate of the Finnish Karelians received little notice outside the country. Yet there was no parallel elsewhere to the voluntary and spontaneous exodus of the province's entire population; it was induced neither by persuasion on the part of the Finnish authorities nor by force or terror on the part of the Russians. The manner in which the Karelians were received was also unique. They were not herded into camps but were billeted, family by family, on the rest of the population throughout the country. And they were compensated for their loss of property, not only in money but also in land for those who were farmers. The resettlement and absorption of the Karelians placed on the Finnish economy an immense burden that is almost impossible to calculate in terms of money. But the social and political gains were equally incalculable. In a relatively short space of time, six to eight years, the Finns who had lost their homes as a result of the war were reintegrated into society. As a consequence, the Karelian issue was virtually removed from the agenda of Finnish-Soviet relations.

The resettlement was accomplished without any foreign assistance. In 1947 the Finnish government reluctantly decided to decline the invitation to join the Marshall Plan so as to avoid arousing Soviet suspicions. It was a decision that cost the country many millions of dollars, but probably did more than anything else to reinforce the credibility of Paasikivi's policy in the eyes of the Soviet leaders. The Marshall Plan was designed to save Europe from communism, but Finland may have saved itself from communism by saying no to the Marshall Plan.

A less tangible but in a sense even more painful act of appeasement was the trial and conviction of eight leading politicians held responsible for Finland's entry into the war against the Soviet Union. This was done in 1946 under a special retroactive law, a procedure that ran contrary to the fundamental concepts of justice prevailing in Finland, and was as repugnant to the judges as it was to the accused. Both sides played their role in the trial in the spirit of national service, acting in the belief that such a sacrifice of principle was part of the price Finland had to pay to retain control of its own affairs. If anyone had to be punished for Finland's wartime policies, better that it be carried out by Finland itself—the only European country engaged in World War II that made the transition from war to peace without a single execution.

The eight men accused of responsibility for Finland's wartime policy were sentenced to prison terms ranging from two to ten years, and all were released after serving half their term. In the eyes of the majority of the people, they were never dishonored. When former president Risto Ryti, who had received the longest sentence of 10 years, died in 1956, he was given a state funeral, at which his successor, President Urho Kekkonen, spoke of his selfless service to his country. Former prime minister Edwin Linkomies, a professor of Latin and Greek, became rector of Helsinki University, and the Social Democratic leader, Väinö Tanner, returned to Parliament and in 1957 was reelected chairman of his party.

There can be no doubt that the Finnish performance, especially the prompt deliveries of the reparations, impressed the men in the Kremlin. But in the West, Paasikivi's faith in a policy of seeking salvation through good works was rejected as naive. As the wartime alliance was coming apart, perceptions of Soviet policy rapidly changed. According to the new conventional wisdom, the Soviet Union was an aggressive, expansionist power that, far from being in need of security itself, was bent upon imposing Communist rule throughout Europe—by subversion if possible, by military conquest if necessary. In 1948 Ernest Bevin, the British foreign secretary, warned his cabinet that Moscow was "planning physical control of the Eurasian land mass and eventual control of the world: no less a thing than that."[3] Such a power could not be appeased; it could only be contained by force. True, Finland had not been turned into a Communist satellite, an awkward fact for people with tidy minds. But surely sooner or later, sooner rather than later, this oversight would be put right.

## The Finnish-Soviet Treaty

Early in 1948 the moment of truth seemed to have arrived. On February 23 President Paasikivi received a personal letter from Stalin. Finland, Stalin pointed out, was the only European neighbor with which the Soviet Union had not yet made a defense agreement against a recurrence of German aggression. He wished to know whether Finland was prepared to conclude with the Soviet Union a treaty of mutual assistance similar to the treaties the Soviet Union had earlier concluded with Hungary and Romania.[4]

The date of the letter was significant. February 23 was the day on which the Communist bid for power in Czechoslovakia was reaching its climax. Western opinion was in a state of shock. When Stalin's letter to Paasikivi was made public a few days later, it became immediately linked in the minds of Western observers with the Communist coup d'état in Prague. The two events were regarded as a concerted advance of international communism upon the remnants of Western democracy in the Soviet sphere of influence. The interests of the Soviet state and the international Communist movement were seen to fuse into a vast conspiracy moving with perfect precision and coordination toward its goal of world domination.

Stalin's stated purpose of creating a defense against future German aggression was dismissed as an obvious pretext. Germany, divided, occupied, and disarmed, was in ruins: what was there to fear? The real purpose of the proposed treaty with Finland, it was believed, was to provide a legal excuse for establishing military bases or moving troops into Finland, not to repel German aggression but to destroy Finnish democracy. It was taken for granted that the Finns had no choice but to submit. Stalin's letter was regarded not as a proposal for negotiations but as a command to be obeyed. Finland as an independent state was speedily written off in the West. The Western powers would do nothing to save Finland, but they could begin to organize themselves to defend a line west of Finland.

From Moscow, the European scene looked different. In the Soviet view, the Marshall Plan was primarily a means of restoring the strength of Germany as a spearhead of an anti-Soviet coalition. Having twice in a lifetime seen the Russian state come close to destruction through German aggression, the Soviet leaders were obsessed with the danger of a resurrection of German power. Throughout the 1930s Soviet diplomacy had labored in vain to induce Russia's western neighbors to agree on security arrangements against Germany, and the lessons of the war had only confirmed, in Soviet eyes, the need for such arrangements. During the war years, mutual assistance pacts had been concluded with

Czechoslovakia and Poland. In February 1948 similar pacts were signed with Hungary and Romania. A pact with Bulgaria would follow in March.

As for Finland, the Soviet wish for a defense pact had been discussed for the first time in the secret Soviet-Finnish talks in 1938–1939. During the war the Soviet government had asked the British as early as 1942 to give advance approval of its plan to conclude a mutual defense treaty with Finland.

After the war, the first initiative for defense talks between Finland and the Soviet Union had been taken by Marshal Mannerheim in the beginning of 1945. As a former Russian general, he had looked at Finland from the other side of the hill. He believed his country's independence could be strengthened if it could be shown that Finland was prepared to serve the defensive needs of its neighbor. Moscow did not respond at the time, presumably because Finland's status had not yet been confirmed by a peace treaty. But soon after this had been done, the Soviet government took up the issue of a defense pact with Finland, first during the visit of a Finnish delegation to Moscow in November 1947, then more formally in Stalin's letter to Paasikivi.

To President Paasikivi, the idea of a treaty with the Soviet Union was not unacceptable in itself. Indeed, the logic of his own policy impelled him to agree to an arrangement that would satisfy the "legitimate interests" of the Soviet Union. But he found the models offered by Stalin wholly unacceptable. The Soviet treaties with Hungary and Romania imposed on the parties an unlimited obligation to political consultations in time of peace and automatic mutual assistance in the event of war. Such a treaty would have made Finland an ally of the Soviets in any and all conflicts between East and West. An overwhelming majority of the Finnish people were totally opposed to an alliance with the Soviet Union—or with any other major power. If there is one dominant theme in Finland's foreign policy, it is the desire to avoid being drawn into conflicts and controversies between more powerful nations. Paasikivi thus had to try to persuade Stalin to be content with an arrangement that, while satisfying Soviet security requirements, would enable Finland to stay outside the two opposing military alliances that were taking shape in Europe.

The Finnish president moved with majestic deliberation. Before making Stalin's letter public, he informed the government and the chairmen of the parliamentary groups. This took five days. On

February 27 he sent Stalin a brief acknowledgment pointing out that in Finland a treaty with a foreign power needed parliamentary approval and therefore the representatives of the people had to be consulted. On March 5 he received the written views of the parliamentary groups. It took him another four days to appoint a delegation for the negotiations with the Soviet Union. On March 9 he replied to Stalin suggesting that the negotiations be held in Moscow. Another nine days passed before the instructions of the Finnish negotiators had been drawn up and approved by the president. On March 20 most members of the delegation traveled to Moscow by train, and its head, Prime Minister Mauno Pekkala, left four days later by plane. On March 25, more than a month after the receipt of Stalin's letter, the first meeting between representatives of Finland and the Soviet Union took place in Moscow.

The timetable of the Finnish preparations, eloquent in itself, was an assertion of Finnish independence and a demonstration of the democratic process. It reassured the Finnish people that their interests were not going to be signed away by frightened men in hasty and secret deals. The president himself stayed in the capital so as not to commit his prestige in advance. He noted in his diary that he did not want to share the fate of prewar Czech president Hacha, who in 1938 suffered a heart attack after being bullied by Hitler to cede Sudetenland without resistance. Parliament was fully consulted, not only before the negotiations but at each subsequent stage. As Paasikivi put it, it was better to fail to reach an agreement in Moscow than to sign a treaty that would be rejected by the Parliament.

The elaborate process of consultations also served another purpose. It displayed the strong opposition that existed in Finland to any kind of defense treaty. Instead of calling in reserves as had been done in October 1939, Paasikivi mobilized the Parliament to back up his negotiating position. Of the three parties represented in the coalition government then in power, only the Communists were prepared to support the kind of treaty Stalin had proposed; the Social Democrats and the Agrarian Party both declared their opposition to a treaty containing military clauses that might involve the country in international conflicts. Opinion among the opposition parties was against even entering negotiations with Moscow.

As the Finnish delegation left Helsinki, rumors of an impending Communist attempt to seize power began to circulate. The stage seemed to be set for a double squeeze—external pressure combined with internal subversion—to put an end to the independence of Finland. Once again, as in the beginning of the century, the cry was "Finis Finlandiae."

After all the alarms and anxieties, the encounter in Moscow was an anticlimax. The Soviet leaders readily agreed to set aside the models suggested in Stalin's letter and asked the Finns to put forward their own suggestions. The Finnish draft was then accepted as the basis for negotiations, and the final text conformed in all essentials to Paasikivi's concept of Finland's role as Russia's neighbor.

At the Kremlin banquet celebrating the signing of the treaty on April 6, 1948, an episode revealed the sense of relief felt by the Finnish negotiators. Stalin the host spoke of the compromise reached in the talks. "What compromise?" interrupted one of the Finns. "The treaty was dictated by Paasikivi." After a moment of stunned silence, Stalin burst out laughing. The Finn who spoke was Urho Kekkonen, the man who would succeed Paasikivi as president a few years later.

The treaty was unique among the scores of security arrangements made between big powers and smaller states in the period after World War II. Its first article states that "should either Finland, or the Soviet Union through the territory of Finland, become the object of military aggression on the part of Germany or any other power allied with Germany, Finland will, true to its duty as a sovereign state, fight to repel aggression." Finnish forces would be acting only within the limits of Finland's own boundaries. The Soviet Union would extend to Finland assistance "if necessary" and "as mutually agreed between the parties": as interpreted by the Finnish Parliament, any agreement on military assistance or military cooperation with the Soviet Union would constitute an independent treaty that would have to be judged on its merits with regard to possible parliamentary approval.

Commenting on the treaty in a broadcast speech to the Finnish people on April 9, 1948, Paasikivi pointed out that the first article really was a statement of the obvious: it described what in any case would happen in the event of an attack against Finland. The obligation to hold consultations between the two parties was narrowed down to cases where a threat of the kind of military aggression described in the first article had been found to exist. And according to Paasikivi, both countries had to agree that there was such a threat.

The treaty thus lacked the essential characteristics of a treaty of alliance, such as regular consultations in time of peace and automatic mutual assistance in case of war. It had been drafted, as was stated in the preamble, "taking into account Finland's desire to stay outside the conflicts and interests between the great powers"—that is, Finland's neutrality. Accordingly, Paasikivi was able to state in his commentary that "Finland had in principle the right to stay neutral in a war between other states."

At the time Finland's aspirations to neutrality were still severely handicapped. As the president himself put it, the lease of the Porkkala military base held by the Soviet Union by virtue of the peace treaty, as well as its right of free transit through Finnish territory to and from Porkkala, "lent Finnish neutrality a colour of its own which did not quite fit the handbooks of international law." But as a clue to the future, the neutrality clause in the preamble of the treaty had a vital importance.

Why did the Soviet government so readily accept the Finnish draft for the treaty? One explanation that suggests itself is that, once again, the time gained by Paasikivi's slow tempo had strengthened the Finnish position. In the four weeks that had elapsed between Stalin's letter and the beginning of the talks in Moscow, the world had changed. The Western powers, shocked into action by the events in Czechoslovakia, had taken a long step toward organizing their common defense. President Harry Truman had promised U.S. support for every country defending its freedom. NATO was being conceived. In the north, Norway was about to abandon its traditional neutrality; even in Sweden defense measures were intensified. At the same time, although this was not then known to outsiders, Stalin's quarrel with Tito was coming to a head. The Soviet leaders could hardly have wished to take on more trouble.

But there could be a simpler explanation. The Finnish-Soviet treaty resembled closely the proposals made by the Soviet government exactly 10 years earlier. It represented a long-term objective of the Soviet Union. After the experiences of the Winter War, Stalin probably did not expect to get more out of Finland in 1948 than what he had proposed in 1938. He knew well that anything beyond what was finally agreed would have met strong resistance. On the eve of the departure of the Finnish delegation from Moscow, Molotov anxiously enquired whether he could be sure that the treaty as signed would actually be ratified by the Finnish Parliament.

The treaty was ratified on April 28, by a vote of 157 to 11, with 30 absent, but the debate preceding the vote revealed the reluctance and misgivings of many members. It also echoed the internal tension then prevailing in Finland. The rumors of a Communist plan to seize power had prompted the president to order preventive measures. Troops were standing by, the police were alerted, and a gunboat was anchored in Helsinki harbor opposite the presidential residence.

No coup d'état was actually attempted, and later research indicates that none was in fact planned. Documents now available reveal that the Finnish Communist Party at the time was far from being the formidable force it was generally supposed to be. Its leadership was divided, and the signals it received from Moscow were often mixed and obscure. The Soviet head of the Allied Control Commission, Andrei Zdanov, Leningrad party boss and heir apparent to Stalin, had made it clear to the Finnish Communists that, although they could count on Moscow's political support, they should not expect to ride into power behind Soviet tanks. As Valentin Falin later put it, "Stalin did not want any trouble in Finland."[5]

What mattered at the time, however, was that "the whole world" believed that the Communists did plan to take over power and that they had been forestalled by Paasikivi's resolute action. This perception had a profound effect on political developments in Finland. In May, the Communist minister of the interior received a vote of no confidence in Parliament on the ground that he had violated the rights of refugees from the Soviet Union, and he was dismissed by the president. In July, the Communist Party suffered a heavy defeat in parliamentary elections and was left out of the government. Once again, Finnish internal politics mirrored the state of international relations: the grand alliance had broken up; the Cold War had begun.

Now the Social Democratic Party was in power and proceeded without delay to dismantle the Communist-dominated security apparatus. Moscow showed its displeasure in several ways. Soviet media echoed the anguished cries of the Finnish Communists and their attacks against Paasikivi himself, and in the winter of 1949–1950 Finnish-Soviet trade talks were stalled without explanation. But in the spring of 1950, after the reelection of Paasikivi and the appointment of a new coalition government under Urho Kekkonen, the Agrarian leader, a trade agreement was signed, although the Communists were still kept out of government. Stalin had not forgotten the lessons of the Winter War. His faithful servant Molotov told an interviewer 20 years later: "People are very stubborn there [in Finland], very stubborn. We were smart not to annex Finland. It would have been a festering wound."[6]

The difference between Finland and Czechoslovakia in 1948 is revealed by a comparison between the internal conditions in the two countries. Communism was stronger in Czechoslovakia than in Finland. The Czechoslovak party had the support of 40 percent of the voters, the Finnish party 23 percent. In Czechoslovakia, Communists held important positions in the civil service and armed forces; in Finland they had little influence in the central organs of government. Attitudes toward Russia also differed: the Czechs and Slovaks on the whole looked upon the Soviet Union as a friend and ally, the only power that in 1939 had declared its readiness to come to the aid of Czechoslovakia, while most Finns still considered the Soviet Union their arch enemy. Finally, President Paasikivi made it clear he was prepared to take strong action against the Communists; President Eduard Benes gave in to the Communist demands without resistance.

In Czechoslovakia the Communists were strong enough to seize power by their own efforts; in Finland only a massive Soviet intervention by military force could have overthrown the elected government. When Stalin told Tito that as a result of World War II both the Soviet Union and the Western Allies would extend their systems of government as far as their armies would reach, he had not added "but no further." Yet such a rider appears to have guided his actions. He did not move against Tito, and he did not move against Finland. He did not have to move against Czechoslovakia.

On the last day of 1948, Paasikivi noted in his diary: "The Communists' coup in Prague was the most important event of the past year. It opened the eyes in the world. . . . " For Paasikivi himself, 1948 had been a year of triumph. He had been able to demonstrate in action that the "legitimate interests" of the Soviet Union could be satisfied by Finland without giving in to the Communists at home.

The picture of Stalin that emerges from his dealings with Finland in the aftermath of World War II is very different from the one that prevailed in the West. Far from scheming to conquer the world, Stalin was a man on the defensive, anxious to avoid trouble in a small neighboring country that had already been written off by the Western powers. Significantly, he had excluded Mannerheim from the list of those to be tried for "war guilt," presumably so as not to provoke resistance in Finland. I am not suggesting that he had undergone a change of heart, settling down in old age as a benevolent and peace-loving ruler. But I do believe he was very conscious of the weakness of the Soviet Union, a country utterly exhausted by the war effort. As in 1940, Stalin acted with extreme caution to buy time for his country to recover its strength.

Western governments and opinion makers did not, on the whole, draw such conclusions from what had happened in Finland. In hindsight, this was perhaps fortunate, because had they done so, they may have neglected to build up Western strength, with possibly disastrous consequences later on. In the Western view, Finland was odd-man-out among the neighbors of the Soviet Union: what had happened there lacked relevance for the general European situation. The Finnish-Soviet Treaty of 1948 was believed to have firmly pinned down Finland into the Soviet sphere of influence. The fact that Paasikivi had succeeded in changing the wording of the treaty was dismissed as unimportant: legal niceties would not stop the Soviets once they decided to act. Finland had gained a respite, that was all.

Whatever hopes Finns had held for Western support in the defense of democracy were shattered at the Paris peace conference in the autumn of 1946. No distinction was made between Finland and Germany's wartime allies—Italy, Hungary, Romania, and Bulgaria, all of which had been under Fascist regimes. In addition to confirming the material provisions of the armistice agreement, the peace treaty handed down to Finland included a clause enjoining the Finnish government to guarantee its citizens all democratic rights and freedoms. Even during wartime, democratic rights and freedoms had been maintained in Finland to a degree that few of the Allied powers sitting in judgment in Paris could claim to have bettered, least of all of course the Soviet Union. Such cynical disregard for the truth of the Finnish situation deepened the disillusionment of the Finnish public with Western policy. Declarations of ideological solidarity among democracies were revealed as empty rhetoric. The Finnish people knew they were on their own. Making a virtue of necessity, they concluded they were better off on their own.

## Enter Urho Kekkonen

According to Aristotle, a border province must never be consulted on a decision to go to war, presumably because its inhabitants will always tend to be opposed to putting themselves at risk. This may contain the gist of a timeless truth, for similar thoughts can be found in Finnish assessments of the position of their country. "As an outpost of a Western alliance Finland would always be the first to be overrun or sacrificed in a conflict, yet too weak to influence decisions on war and peace," said Urho Kekkonen in 1943. Kekkonen, who later became president, concluded that Finland had to adopt a policy of neutrality, but one that unlike the prewar policy could gain the confidence of the Soviet Union.

For 10 years after the end of World War II, neutrality remained an unspoken aspiration of Finnish policy. Neutrality had no place in Stalin's dogmatic view of a world rigidly divided into two hostile camps: whoever was not for the Soviet Union was against it. With Soviet forces standing guard at Porkkala base, Finland was like a prisoner free on parole. Yet even then, Finland managed to practice a policy of neutrality without actually saying so. Having declined the invitation to join the Marshall Plan on the ground that it had become a matter of dispute between the big powers, President Paasikivi was confronted in November 1954 with an invitation from Soviet foreign minister Molotov to a European security conference. Its purpose, according to the Soviet proposal, was to create a European security system within which Germany could be unified. The invitation had been sent to all European states as well as to the United States and Canada, but it was immediately clear that the West would reject it.

The world watched with interest to see which side Finland would take. The Finnish reply was formally positive: Yes, Finland was in favor of a European security system and would be happy to join the conference of the states invited by Moscow. What was not said but implied was that Finland would join only if all those invited would accept. Because this condition was not fulfilled, Finland did not send a delegation to the Moscow conference, which, as it turned out, was the first formal step toward the creation of the Warsaw Pact.

Another crucial test for Finland was the German issue. The West claimed the government of the Federal Republic of Germany was the sole legitimate representative of the German people as a whole, while the Soviet Union insisted that two separate sovereign German states existed. To recognize only the Federal Republic was to accept the Western claim; to recognize two German states was to side with the Soviet Union and risk economic retaliation from the West. Finland solved the problem in a manner probably unprecedented in the history of international relations; it recognized neither the Federal Republic nor the Democratic Republic. Instead of diplomatic relations, in both states it maintained trade missions that functioned in practice like embassies. Neither side was happy with this arrangement, but both accepted it. For the West, the important thing was that Finland refused to recognize the East German state; the East Germans made the most of the fact that Finland accorded both German states equal treatment. The arrangement was continued until 1972, when the existence of two German states was recognized by the West.

By such evasive maneuvers, the Finnish government stayed uncommitted in a divided Europe. But Finland was not yet recognized as a neutral country, nor did President Paasikivi use that word to define Finland's position. He was very conscious of the shadow cast by the Porkkala base.

Once again, however, a shift in the Kremlin power constellation provided Finland with the chance to break free. After Stalin's death, Nikita Khrushchev gained a dominant position in the Soviet leadership, and he was giving Soviet foreign policy a new look. Now whoever was not against the Soviet Union was a potential friend. He made his peace with Tito and courted India's Jawalharlal Nehru. He returned to China the Soviet bases in Dairen and Port Arthur. In Europe, he began to promote the creation of a neutral zone between the Warsaw Pact and NATO. As a first step, in spring 1955, he agreed to withdraw the Soviet occupation forces from Austria in return for Austria's pledge of neutrality. And in August 1955, President Paasikivi received an offer he could not refuse: the Soviet government was prepared to return to Finland the Porkkala base, provided Finland agreed to extend the validity of the 1948 treaty for another 20 years. Ignoring the Soviet military presence in the Warsaw Pact countries, Khrushchev then claimed that the Soviet Union had given up all its foreign bases and urged the United States to do the same.

In the West, the return of Porkkala was dismissed as a cheap gesture. Obviously, the base had lost its usefulness. By giving it up, the Soviet Union had given up nothing in terms of the global balance of power.

For Finland, however, the departure of the Soviet forces from Porkkala in January 1956 was an event of profound significance. Had the Soviet Union had aggressive designs on Finland, Porkkala could easily have been used for pressure or blackmail. By abandoning the base, Khrushchev showed that the Soviet Union had come to trust Finland to keep its end of the bargain struck in 1948. The concession lent powerful support to Paasikivi's thesis that Soviet policy toward Finland was defensive and that the line he had taken was the best way of securing Finnish independence.

The return of the Soviet base transformed Finland's international position. There was an obvious parallel to Soviet actions in Austria and in Finland in 1955. In the case of Austria, Moscow agreed to withdraw its occupation forces on the condition that Austria commit itself to neutrality; in the case of Finland, the return of the base enabled Finland to claim neutrality. As long as the Finnish government did not have full control over its territory, it had not been in the position to ask other states to respect its neutrality in the event of war. The removal of the Soviet base opened the way toward international recognition of Finnish neutrality. It followed from Khrushchev's larger design that he was the first foreign leader to call Finland a neutral state. This happened at the Twentieth Congress of the Soviet Communist Party in February 1956, an occasion remembered primarily for Khrushchev's "secret" speech in which he revealed Stalin's crimes.

At this time Finland also joined the Nordic Council, a joint body of the parliaments of the Nordic countries, which was the main forum for economic and social cooperation in the region. Although security issues were excluded from its agenda, formal recognition of Finland's membership in the Nordic family had an immense psychological importance for the Finnish people. Significantly, Khrushchev did not object. No doubt he believed Finland would influence the other Nordic countries in the direction of neutrality.

The famous thaw in Soviet policy raised great expectations. Even Secretary of State John Foster Dulles, who a few years earlier had called neutrality an immoral position for a free nation to take, was all for neutrality on the other side of the dividing line. In American comments, the Finnish example was believed to transmit muted signals of hope for the "captive nations" of Eastern Europe. If Finland could be neutral without posing a risk to Soviet security, why not Hungary or Czechoslovakia or Poland?

Obviously, the question was asked in Moscow too. In conversations with Finnish leaders, Khrushchev later revealed that the withdrawal of Soviet forces from Porkkala and from Austria had been opposed by Molotov and other hard-liners. Khrushchev's critics must have felt grim satisfaction when news of the Hungarian declaration of neutrality reached Moscow. In October 1956, as Soviet tanks were crushing the Hungarian freedom fighters, Khrushchev's vision of a neutral zone separating NATO and the Warsaw Pact turned into a nightmare. East-West relations were frozen over once again. But by then Porkkala was safely in Finnish hands.

There was, however, more to the Soviet move on Porkkala than meets the eye: a plot within the plot. In addition to serving as evidence of the Soviet desire for peace with the West, the return of the base was used to promote the political fortunes of Urho Kekkonen, then prime minister and candidate of the Agrarian Party to succeed President Paasikivi. Elections were to be held in February 1956, and Soviet diplomacy made every effort to present Kekkonen as a key figure in the negotiations for the return of the base. They coined the phrase "Paasikivi-Kekkonen line" to describe Finnish foreign policy. Kekkonen himself campaigned as the man best fitted to take over Paasikivi's role as guarantor of good relations with the Soviet Union. And he was elected, although by the narrowest possible margin—151 to 149 votes in the electoral college.

The Soviet efforts to influence the Finnish presidential election reveals a paradox at the heart of the Kremlin. In theory, the Soviet leaders were supposed to be guided by the scientific truths of Marxism-Leninism, according to which politics was determined by the impersonal forces of the class struggle; in practice, they relied on personal relations. Within the Soviet Union, power was based on an intricate web of personal loyalties, a legacy of the Russian tradition, and in their dealings with other countries, the Soviet leaders tended to place their trust in persons rather than in institutions. Disregarding ideological affinities, Moscow looked for the person "you could do business with," as Margaret Thatcher said after her first meeting with Mikhail Gorbachev in 1985: the person who could deliver his end of whatever deal had been made. In Finland this man was first Mannerheim, then Paasikivi, both arch-conservatives, and after Paasikivi it was to be Kekkonen. He too was a man firmly committed to preserving the Finnish democratic system. The Finnish constitution grants the president wide powers, including the authority to direct foreign policy.

In September 1960, to refute suspicions that he was "soft on Communism," Kekkonen said that even if all the rest of Europe were to go Communist, the Finnish people would stick to their system of government. In an added twist, the statement was made in a luncheon speech at the Soviet embassy in the presence of Nikita Khrushchev, who was visiting Helsinki. But the Soviet leader had the last word. In that case, he replied, Finland would be like an outdoor museum where the Soviets would send their young people to see what capitalism had been like.

The exchange echoed the famous 1959 "kitchen debate" between Khrushchev and U.S. vice president Richard Nixon in Moscow. "Your grand-children will live under Communism!" Khrushchev had shouted. Today, all this sounds merely quaint. At the time, however, Khrushchev's prediction touched a sensitive nerve in the West. An influential segment of opinion makers tended to use a double standard in judging the merits of the two competing systems—capitalism by its actual performance, communism by its promise of a better future. The Soviet "Sputnik" and the imagined "missile gap" between the United States and the Soviet Union had shaken the West's self-confidence. Kekkonen liked to quote what Allen Dulles, the CIA chief, had told him during his visit to Washington in October 1961. Dulles had compared the ideological contest to a wrestling match between an aging champion grown soft and flabby with success and a lean and hungry challenger. Kekkonen seemed to share this assessment.

Although Kekkonen presented himself as the heir of Paasikivi's policy, the two men were different in practically every respect. As a member of the conservative establishment, Paasikivi had taken public office for granted. He had never been a candidate in a parliamentary election, and in the 1950 presidential election, his victory had been a foregone conclusion. He was a nineteenth-century man, steeped in history, with a Bismarckian view of the nature of statesmanship.

Urho Kekkonen, born in 1900 in a log cabin (literally), was the son of a lumber company foreman in the backward region of northeastern Finland. His life's story personified the struggles of the Finnish nation in the twentieth century. He worked his way through university and fought his first election campaign as a candidate of the Agrarian Party in 1937. Until the end of his days, he regarded himself as a champion of the poor against the privileged. But he was a nationalist, not a socialist. Social justice and equality were means to make the Finnish nation strong enough to survive as an independent state. A strong state was needed to develop the country's resources and resolve potential conflicts between different groups in the interest of national unity. But a year of study in Nazi Germany cured him of any leaning toward totalitarian methods. Returning home he wrote a pamphlet entitled *Democracy's Self-Defense*, in which he advocated stronger measures against extremists on the right as well as on the left. Appointed minister of the interior in 1937, he proceeded to ban the right-wing movement IKL, but lost his case in court. This made him too controversial to be included in the all-party national coalition formed at the outbreak of the war.

As a frustrated outsider, Kekkonen was one of the few members of Parliament who voted against making peace in March 1940. He argued that Finland should have accepted the offer of aid from Britain and France and continued to fight. When he later learned the truth about the Anglo-French expeditionary force, he was bitterly disillusioned. His feeling that the West had let Finland down colored his outlook for a long time. In June 1941, Kekkonen enthusiastically supported the war against the Soviet Union, but after the German defeat in Stalingrad during the winter of 1942–1943, he experienced something akin to a political conversion. He realized that because Finland could rely neither on the West nor on Germany to protect itself against the Soviets, the nation had to come to terms with the realities of power and find a way to live in friendship with the Soviet Union. This was not an original idea: the government had reached the same conclusion at about the same time. But free of government responsibility, Kekkonen was able to pursue this line with uncompromising consistency, thus positioning himself at the end of the war as a leading advocate of a fundamental reorientation of Finnish policy.

Among Finland's postwar politicians, Urho Kekkonen stood out as a formidable personality. He possessed a prodigious intellectual capacity and the physical energy of a champion athlete. He inspired unquestioning loyalty and devotion among a large following, but also aroused bitter hostility. In the eyes of his supporters he was the only man who could save Finland without another war. His opponents called him an opportunist who had made a Faustian deal with the Kremlin to maintain his personal power.

At this point I must declare my interest. While in the foreign service, I was from the beginning of the 1960s until my resignation at the end of 1974 one of President Kekkonen's closest advisers, an executor of his policies, his spokesman, and occasional "spin doctor." I am probably to some extent still under the spell of his magnetic personality, although repelled by the underhanded methods he used to maintain and exercise power. I cannot claim to be a detached historian of his time.

Kekkonen did not start off with the personal authority his predecessor had had, and during his first period (1956–1962), Finland was convulsed by an internal struggle for power. The opposition claimed that it, too, supported the Paasikivi policy, but did not trust Kekkonen to conduct it in the national interest. But Moscow campaigned for him openly. Soviet leader Nikita Khrushchev declared publicly in 1960 that "whoever is for Kekkonen is for friendship with the Soviet Union and whoever is against Kekkonen is against friendship with the Soviet Union." In October 1961, on the eve of the Finnish presidential election, the Soviet government, claiming that the Berlin crisis had created a threat of war in northern Europe, proposed that Finland and the Soviet Union should hold military consultations in accordance with the 1948 treaty. The Soviet initiative frightened the Finnish people, but turned out to be a godsend for Kekkonen's presidential campaign. He traveled to the Soviet Union to meet Khrushchev, and on his return was able to announce that he had persuaded the Soviet leader to drop his demand. It was widely believed that Kekkonen had saved the country, and he was reelected with a large majority. Was this dramatic crisis in Finnish-Soviet relations just mirrors and smoke—a show put on to make sure Kekkonen would stay in power? The jury of scholars is still looking for clues in the Soviet archives.

From 1962 until his retirement for reasons of health in September 1981, Kekkonen dominated Finland's political life. I believe he was convinced of his mission as the savior of the country's independence: not an uncommon form of megalomania among strong political leaders. I thought of Kekkonen when I read Margaret Thatcher's memoirs. She describes recalling Chatham's famous remark when she entered Number 10 Downing Street: "I know that

I can save this country and that no one else can." Mrs. Thatcher adds: "If I am honest, I must admit my exhilaration came from a similar inner conviction!"[7] Politicians with a mission have one thing in common: they believe they owe it to the nation to stay in power and to use whatever means necessary for this purpose.

The ultimate rationale for Kekkonen's mission, as he saw it, was Finland's exposed situation in the case of a new European war. He was convinced, at any rate during the first two decades of the Cold War, that a conflict between East and West was likely, if not unavoidable. I remember the president's reaction at the height of the 1962 Cuban crisis, when I had to wake him in the middle of the night to inform him of the U.S. decision to blockade Cuba. After a short pause, he said: "Haven't I always said that it is bound to start somewhere." As it happened, he left the following morning for a state visit to France, and at their first meeting President Charles de Gaulle entirely agreed with Kekkonen's somber analysis of the Cuban situation. Both men thrived on crises: the threat of war legitimized their style of leadership.

Because a third world war might destroy the very existence of the nation, Finland had to make sure, according to Kekkonen, that the Soviet leaders would trust the Finns to fulfill their obligations under the 1948 treaty. Government declarations on foreign policy were not enough. As John F. Kennedy once had said, "The line dividing domestic and foreign affairs has become as indistinct as a line drawn in water." Accordingly, Kekkonen insisted that Finnish political life as a whole had to be geared to serve the goal of gaining and keeping the confidence of the Soviet leaders. Time and again, he urged the media to support this effort. Under his leadership, Finland became the very model of "a national security state."

Kekkonen carefully cultivated his personal contacts with the Soviet leaders. Visible access to the Kremlin was his master key to power at home. Like many other modern statesmen, Kekkonen was a firm believer in the magic of personal diplomacy. He got on specially well with Nikita Khrushchev, with whom he shared a radical temperament and a robust sense of humor. There is no doubt that he persuaded Khrushchev to make concessions that other members of the Soviet leadership considered excessive.

Kekkonen's most important achievements during his first term were to bring Finland into the European Free Trade Association in 1961, while preserving the profitable bilateral trade with the

Soviet Union. At the end of the complex negotiations in Moscow, Kekkonen invited Khrushchev and other Soviet leaders, including Anastas Mikoyan, the Politburo member in charge of foreign trade policy, to a luncheon at the Finnish embassy. Khrushchev praised the agreement reached between the two countries as an example of the readiness of the Soviet government to take into consideration the interests of a small neighbor. Suddenly he was interrupted by Mikoyan who shouted: "Even if the small neighbor demands the impossible?" After a few further exchanges, Khrushchev told his colleague to shut up. The incident revealed a glimpse of the inner tensions that a few years later led to Khrushchev's downfall. At a later meeting with Kekkonen, Khrushchev admitted he had been criticized by more orthodox members of the Politburo of being too friendly with "a leader of a capitalist country."

When told in October 1964 of Khrushchev's forced retirement and his replacement by the troika of Brezhnev, Kosygin, and Podgorny, Kekkonen was visibly shaken, but recovered quickly and said: "I used to have a good friend in Moscow; I understand I now have three." Of the three, Prime Minister Aleksei Kosygin came to replace Khrushchev as Kekkonen's closest contact in the Kremlin. Almost each year in the late 1960s and early 1970s, the two men spent several days together fishing or hiking in some remote part of the Soviet Union.

The attention the Soviet leaders paid to Kekkonen clearly went beyond what could be considered normal in the case of the head of state of a small country. I believe they looked upon him as a friendly guide to the mysterious world of capitalism. To the members of the Soviet elite in general, Finland became a testing ground where they could safely practice the art of getting along with Westerners. It also happened to be the best shopping center in the neighborhood.

Kekkonen used his high-level contacts to bypass the heavy-handed Soviet bureaucracy and make sure the Soviet leaders received his version of Finnish policy. He used back channels provided by the KGB to keep in touch with the Kremlin, often leaving the Finnish government and the foreign ministry in the dark about his dealings. No doubt he was confident that the Kremlin would protect its secrets forever. Now that Soviet archives have been partially opened, the tricky game Kekkonen played is coming under scrutiny by Finnish historians. But he was convinced that his were the most effective methods for dealing with the Kremlin. Kekkonen angrily rejected the charge that he undermined Finland's independence by giving the Soviets a say in internal Finnish affairs. On the contrary, he would say, Finnish independence was safeguarded by his prudent policy. Finland could not afford the luxury of self-satisfying gestures that might provoke the powerful neighbor.

## The Dag Hammarskjöld Syndrome

"Finnish neutrality is the essence of my life's work," President Kekkonen declared in November 1961. "I will defend it to my last breath." To an outsider, such a passionate commitment to what commonly is considered a posture of cool detachment may seem strange. But to the Finnish people at the time it did not sound strange at all. Kekkonen made his statement in the shadow of the Berlin crisis. Moscow had just invited the Finnish government to enter in military consultations, and it was widely feared that this was merely a pretext for a Soviet attempt to put an end to Finnish independence. Kekkonen's pledge to defend Finnish neutrality was his way of saying no. He said "neutrality," but every Finn understood he meant independence.

Neutrality always implies the rejection of another alternative. The position of Sweden during the Cold War is a case in point. By staying neutral Sweden said no to NATO. It followed that the Western powers regarded Swedish neutrality with displeasure, while the Soviet Union praised it. As Machiavelli put it, "The one who is not your friend will want you to remain neutral, and the one who is your friend, will require you to declare yourself by taking arms."[8]

There were no identical twins among the neutral countries in Europe. Austria's road to neutrality was unique. By adopting permanent neutrality, Austria persuaded the Soviet Union to agree to end the occupation. From the Soviet point of view, Austrian neutrality was in effect a commitment not to join Germany: no second Anschluss. In time, neutrality became part of Austria's identity as a separate nation—separate, that is, from Germany.

Finland's position differed fundamentally from that of the other neutral states in Europe. In a formal sense, the difference was that it had a security treaty with the Soviet Union, while the other neutral states had no such treaty commitments. In fact, however, we now know that Sweden had secretly made elaborate arrangements with NATO to receive military assistance in the event of a Soviet attack. In contrast, the unspoken goal of Finnish policy was to do everything possible to avoid accepting Soviet military assistance. The real difference between the two countries was that Sweden could implicitly depend on the support of the Western community to which it belonged, while Finland's security policy had to be divorced from the country's ideological, cultural, and economic ties with the Western world.

Neutrality was designed to resolve the latent conflict between ideology and strategy. Like the ancient deity Janus, Finland wore two faces. To the West, the message was: We are neutral, that means we are an independent democracy, not a Soviet satellite. But we have to be careful, so don't make our life more difficult than it already is. And to the East: We are neutral; that means we will not join your enemies, and if they try to attack you through Finland, we will defend ourselves, and we can do it—or have you forgotten?

The improvement in East-West relations that set in after the 1962 Cuban crisis opened the way for Finland to move from its evasive line of neutrality to a more active role on the international scene. All the neutral countries were anxious to persuade the world that their policy was not merely a way of saving their own skin, but actually served the higher interests of the international community. A neutral country is able to provide such useful services as mediation or peacekeeping forces, and it can make out-of-the-way meeting places available to the leaders of the big powers. By making itself useful, a neutral country reinforces its own neutrality. Thus, like Narcissus, a neutral country draws strength from its own image. Each hopes to be recognized as another Switzerland marked by a protective red cross on the maps of the strategists of the big powers.

For Finland, a more active policy had a more specific purpose. It was designed to overcome Western skepticism of Finland's ability to maintain a genuinely neutral position between East and West, without at the same time arousing suspicions in Moscow. The United Nations offered a natural arena for this delicate diplomatic exercise. In the mid-1960s the superpowers were discovering the usefulness of the United Nations. The Soviet leaders were obsessed with what they perceived to be a deadly threat from Mao's China and were seeking tacit U.S. support against "the yellow peril." Americans were preoccupied with the war in Vietnam; they, too, believed China to be the main obstacle to peace. The Cuban crisis had taught both to be wary of Third World conflicts that might get out of hand. The UN could provide facilities for the joint management of such conflicts. Thus détente stimulated demand for the kind of services the neutral countries were keen on offering. As Finnish ambassador to the UN in 1965–1972, my job was to make sure that Finland gained its share of this market.

In the UN, the Nordic countries worked in close unity. This privileged little group of politically stable, socially advanced, prosperous countries that have no major international claims to press or to counter, no present or recent colonial record, and no racial problems represents moderation and rationality in an organization often swayed by fanatic or neurotic forces: model members of the UN, as Secretary-General U Thant once called them. During the Cold War, the Nordic countries contributed military personnel to almost every peacekeeping operation mounted by the UN, and they still maintain permanent standby forces so as to be able to respond promptly to a request for peacekeeping services. More mediators have been recruited from their ranks than from any other comparable group of states.

The Nordic commitment to the UN is still influenced by what could be called the Dag Hammarskjöld syndrome. Hammarskjöld, the Swedish diplomat who served as UN secretary-general from 1952 to 1961, personified the Nordic vision of a rational world order. Although he is not widely remembered today, I believe his extraordinary effort to turn the office of secretary-general into an autonomous actor in world politics—an effort that ended in political failure and personal tragedy—carries a lesson that is still relevant.

How Hammarskjöld came to be appointed secretary-general in 1952 is a story abounding in irony. He did not seek the office, and those who selected him had no intention of launching him onto a spectacular career. The big powers at the time were tired of the political pretensions of Tryggve Lie, the first secretary-general; they wanted a faceless bureaucrat to run the Secretariat, and Dag Hammarskjöld, a neutral civil servant from neutral Sweden, seemed perfect for the part.

For a while Hammarskjöld did concentrate, as was expected of him, on his administrative duties. But in 1955 his successful initiative in negotiating the release of U.S. airmen captured in China gave him a taste of independent political action, and the Suez crisis in 1956 propelled him into the center of the world stage. On his reappointment for a second term in 1957, Hammarskjöld was ready to put forward a revolutionary concept of the role of the secretary-general. In his view, the secretary-general should act independently to fill any "vacuum" created by the failure of the powers to agree on issues affecting world peace. Because he had no means of power at his disposal, he had to rely on such innovative devices as the UN peacekeeping force in the Suez, observers in Lebanon, and a "presence" in Laos.

For a few moments in history, the secretary-general did become an autonomous influence in world politics representing, in his own words, "the detached element in international life." He claimed the UN was "the main protector of the interests of those many nations who feel themselves strong as members of the international family but who are weak in isolation." In his famous rebuttal of Khrushchev's charges of partiality, Hammarskjöld pointed out that it was not the Soviet Union or any other big power who needed the United Nations for their protection, but "all the others." To the new states emerging from colonial rule, Hammarskjöld offered the services of the UN as a shield against the predatory designs of the two rival blocs.[9]

Hammarskjöld's last year at the UN can now be seen as an effort to transform the organization from an organ of cooperation between sovereign states into an instrument of the membership's collective responsibility—a heroic effort doomed to failure. True, a convincing case can be made to prove that, on balance, Hammarskjöld maintained impartiality between West and East. But it was a mistake to believe that the governments of the big powers would judge him by some abstract or objective criteria. Khrushchev or de Gaulle was not likely to say to himself, "This time Hammarskjöld went against us, but it is only fair, last time he was with us." They judged him by the political consequences of his actions in each concrete case separately. When his actions in the former Belgian Congo (later Zaire, now Congo again) went against Soviet interests, Moscow turned on him, and it did not help him that France, Belgium, and Britain were also dissatisfied with what he was doing there. The big powers were prepared to support him only as long as both sides in the Cold War could benefit from what he did. The United Nations was never meant to limit the freedom of action of its principal founding members.

Hammarskjöld's failure revealed the limits of the usefulness of neutral mediation in international conflicts. It is helpful when the parties to a dispute have the will to reach a settlement. In the absence of such a will, the kind of services the UN can provide can at best help contain the conflict. The UN efforts in the Middle East are a case in point. After the six-day war in 1967, the Swedish diplomat Gunnar Jarring was appointed special representative of the secretary-general—significantly the Arab states rejected the term mediator—to help the parties to reach a settlement. He shuttled for quite some time between Jerusalem and the Arab capitals, but to no avail. But when Henry Kissinger appeared on the scene things began to happen. "Aren't you afraid that Kissinger will say one thing in Cairo and another in Jerusalem?" I asked my Egyptian colleague. He looked at me pityingly: "But of course he does," he replied. Kissinger was not an honest broker. He was an enforcer of U.S. policy, with the power to reward and punish. A more recent case is of course Bosnia, where finally the use of force was needed to put an end to the fighting. In the Iraq crisis of March 1998, Secretary-General Kofi Annan was able to negotiate an agreement with Saddam Hussein because he was backed by a credible threat of U.S. military action.

These are afterthoughts not voiced at the time of East-West détente in the 1960s. That the neutral countries played a useful role in softening the confrontation between the two military blocs was generally accepted. As the fear of war lessened, the climate of opinion changed in Europe. With memories of Stalin's terror fading, the Soviet Union appeared to many Europeans not as an aggressive expansionist power, but rather as a defender of stability; a repressive society, but less so than before; less developed than the West but slowly improving its standard of living in conditions of social security. Belief in an inevitable convergence between the two systems was gaining ground. It was encouraged by the Communist parties in Western Europe that were beginning to break out of the Stalinist mold.

## The Communist Split

In Finland, too, attitudes were changing. All Communists were no longer regarded as agents of a foreign power or advocates of violent revolution. A majority among the Communists themselves were desperately anxious to prove themselves as good Finns and democrats.

In 1966, President Kekkonen decided to give them a chance

to do so. After 18 years in opposition, the Communist Party was accepted as a partner in a coalition government with the Social Democratic Party and the Center Party (formerly the Agrarian Party). In a speech in February 1967, Kekkonen pointed out that, just as peaceful cooperation in international relations meant increasing cooperation between states with different social systems, it should be possible to cooperate internally with the Communists in a spirit of peaceful competition between different ideologies. He could not accept the view that every fifth voter must be regarded as unpatriotic. Treating the Communists as outcasts could only drive them further into hostility. The time had come, Kekkonen declared, "to integrate" the Communists into Finnish society. This could only be achieved by allowing them to take part in political life on an equal footing with the other parties.

Kekkonen at the time believed in convergence. He wrote in a letter in 1963: "I am neither a Hegelian nor a Marxist, but I do believe that the historical trend is towards a synthesis replacing the present struggle [between the two systems]." His analysis antici-pated the emergence of the trend within the Communist movement that later became known as "Eurocommunism." But his opening to the Left was received with many misgivings, in Finland as well as in the West. Few Western observers were prepared to share Kekkonen's assumption that the Communists would be ready to put national interest first and abide by the rules of the parliamentary game. Ominously, Moscow welcomed the entry of the Communists into the Finnish government. The Soviet line at the time was to encourage the Communist parties in Western Europe to break out of their isolation and join other "peace loving forces" in a modern version of the Popular Front. This looked like a maneuver designed to undermine Western unity from within. Eurocommunism, in this view, was the Trojan horse by which the enemies of NATO would be smuggled into the governments of such countries as Italy or France; once inside, they would cling to power by any means.

What actually happened was something neither Kekkonen nor his critics had foreseen. Eurocommunism did begin to undermine the rigid structure of Europe—but on the Eastern side of the divid-ing line. The Prague Spring showed what convergence meant in practice: a movement in one direction only, away from the Soviet model. The occupation of Czechoslovakia by Warsaw Pact forces in the autumn of 1968 put an end for almost 20 years to all efforts to reform the Soviet system from within. It also uncovered the deep cracks in the very foundations of the international Communist movement.

George Kennan happened to be in Helsinki the day the Soviet tanks rolled into Prague. The next morning President Kekkonen invited him and me for a talk. Kennan's comment was that this was the beginning of the end of the international Communist movement. "But Finland is safe," Kekkonen remarked, "because we are not part of the Socialist system." Both remarks proved to be true.

The occupation of Czechoslovakia revealed once and for all the fallacy in the speculation often voiced by Western commentators that Finland might serve as a model for a more tolerant Soviet policy toward its satellites. Henry Kissinger, for instance, has asked whether Stalin's fallback position for Eastern Europe was a status similar to Finland's.[10] In fact, from Moscow's point of view, Finland and Poland and the other satellites belonged to different categories—capitalist and socialist; there was no halfway station between them. If Poland had become "more like Finland," the entire power structure in Eastern Europe would have been undermined. Thus, the reform movement in Czechoslovakia had to be stopped because it would have spread to the other satellite countries and eventually into the Soviet Union itself, endangering centralized political control, at home as well as in the outer empire. The process was reversed 20 years later. Having initiated reform in the Soviet Union, Gorbachev had no choice but to let the satellite countries go their own way. Using force to stop them would have meant an end to reform in the Soviet Union itself.

In Finland, the immediate effect of the events in Czechoslovakia was to split the Communist Party wide open between the dogmatists who insisted the Soviet Union could do no wrong and the reformers who believed that every Communist Party had the right to follow its own road in accordance with national requirements. The latter were clearly in majority, but the Soviet Union supported the minority faction: no number of votes could undo the sin of heresy.

The problem for President Kekkonen turned out to be not how to get the Communists out of the government, but how to keep them in and make them share responsibility for unpopular economic policies. Participation in a coalition government means making compromises, and compromise is alien to a revolutionary party. The dogmatists feared, quite rightly, that continued cooperation with the other parties would ultimately lead to a loss of identity, making the Communist Party a mere annex to Social Democracy. But the only alternative they could offer was withdrawal into sterile opposition. The dilemma was insoluble; either way the party was doomed to loose influence and support.

The policy of self-destruction pursued by the Finnish Communist Party in the 1970s was carefully noted by François Mitterrand, the French Socialist leader, as I realized when I met him in Paris in 1978. Turning aside all other subjects, he questioned me closely on what had happened to the Finnish Communists. After his victory in the presidential election in 1979, Mitterrand effectively used the Finnish recipe to divide and weaken the French Communist Party.

## The European Security Conference

Finland was safe, as Kekkonen had said, safe from communism. Yet, in a roundabout way, the occupation of Czechoslovakia did affect Finland's position. The Prague Spring had revealed to the Soviet leaders what kind of forces détente might release within the Soviet bloc itself. The Kremlin's response was to close down all hatches. With regard to Finland, this meant a revision of the policy Khrushchev had adopted in the mid-1950s. Finnish neutrality now seemed to offer a dangerous temptation to Eastern European countries. In 1969 the Soviet government refused to describe Finland as a neutral country in a joint communiqué, insisting on giving the 1948 Finnish-Soviet treaty priority. What followed was a long-drawn-out battle of words, like a medieval scholastic dispute, fought between the officials who draft the sacred texts of diplomatic declarations. Finally a convoluted compromise was reached: both the 1948 treaty and Finland's policy of neutrality were mentioned in a single paragraph—in that order. In practice nothing of substance changed, but the implications were ominous. Finland's future position in the European system was at stake.

The Soviet proposal, made in 1969, to convene a European security conference became a crucial test for Finland. The Soviet objective was clear: the purpose of the conference was to legitimize the territorial and political changes brought about by World War II. The West was asked to ratify the Soviet version of the Monroe Doctrine. In the Soviet view, explicit acceptance of the status quo was essential to ensure peace in Europe. Ambiguity in Western attitudes to the borders or the regimes in Eastern Europe kept alive hopes of change, and this bred insecurity. The dangerous consequences had been seen in Hungary in 1956 and in Czechoslovakia in 1968. Stability, according to Moscow, was a key to peace and security and a precondition to cooperation between East and West.

Finland, too, was in favor of stability based on the status quo—provided that Finland's status as a neutral country was clearly recognized as part of the European system. It was thus in our interest to support the Soviet proposal. The problem was how to make sure our condition would be understood by all concerned. I can claim to have played a role in resolving this problem, for it was on my suggestion that the Finnish government decided to take an initiative of its own by proposing that the security conference be held in Helsinki, the only European capital where both German states were represented on an equal footing. The Finnish proposal also included the suggestion that, in addition to all European states, the United States and Canada be invited to the conference. This was something the Soviets at the time had not yet publicly conceded.

The Finnish initiative served a dual purpose. One was to advertise Finland's independent position; the other, to nail down the Finnish policy on Germany, which was under constant pressure from the Soviet side. In Soviet eyes, the Finnish move was a subterfuge, like a guerrilla action behind their own lines, but there was nothing they could do about it without undermining their own campaign for the conference.

In July–August 1975 the Conference on Security and Cooperation in Europe (CSCE) adopted its Final Act in Helsinki. In Finnish eyes, the gathering of 35 heads of state or government in the Finnish capital was the grand finale of Finland's long labors to gain international recognition of its status as a neutral country. Finnish neutrality, President Kekkonen noted, was thus firmly embedded into the European structure.

The general significance of the Helsinki conference is still a matter of debate. Realists in the West dismissed it as a show without substance, mere figure skating on the hard surface of reality, designed to lull the West into lowering its guard and so to weaken the real foundation for peace and security—the balance of military power. Lately, a more benign view has gained ground. The Helsinki conference is said to have sown the seeds of freedom within the Soviet empire. No doubt the chapter on human rights in the Final Act signed in Helsinki encouraged dissidents in the satellite countries and even in the Soviet Union itself, but it seems to be wishful thinking to believe that they played a major role in bringing down the Soviet system.

The immediate impact of the Helsinki conference at any rate was quite different. With West German chancellor Helmut Schmidt and East German Communist leader Erich Honecker sitting side by side as custodians of the holy status quo, the conference was a major triumph for Soviet policy. The existence of two German states had finally been recognized by the whole world. As Foreign Minister Andrei Gromyko had declared, no longer could any important international issue be settled without the participation of the Soviet Union. The Soviet leaders clearly believed "the correlation of forces" in the world had shifted decisively in their favor—an assessment widely accepted among Western analysts. The respected U.S. scholar Adam Ulam, for instance, wrote in 1976 that "the Soviet Union under Brezhnev had achieved the leading, if not yet dominant position in world politics."

The self-confidence of the Western world had been shattered by the oil crisis in 1973. Western societies were wracked with self-doubt, guilt about the past, and pessimism about the future. The Soviet Union, in contrast, seemed to stand for stability and order, confident in its ability to sustain a steady improvement in living standards under conditions of social equality and security. To the leaders of many countries in the Third World, the Soviet Union offered a superior model of economic progress under social control, as well as a source of military assistance. The ominous growth of Soviet military power loomed ever larger. At the Helsinki conference, Western Europe accepted, with relief, a European settlement on Soviet terms, leaving the United States to face the expansion of Soviet influence and power in the Third World.

The Final Act of the CSCE signed in Helsinki explicitly recognized the right of states to choose neutrality. Yet, for Finland, the Final Act was not the last word. In July 1978, Soviet defense minister Dimitri Ustinov startled his hosts during an official visit to Finland by taking up for discussion an issue that a few days before his arrival had been raised in the newspaper of the Stalinist wing of the Finnish Communist Party. The paper had suggested that, since the 1948 treaty envisaged the possibility of joint action for the defense of Finnish territory, it would be useful to arrange joint Finnish-Soviet military exercises in preparation for such an eventuality.

Anyone with a reasonable understanding of Finnish policy

could have told Ustinov that this would be totally unacceptable to Finland, and in fact President Kekkonen refused to enter into any discussion on the subject. As was pointed out later by the Finnish defense minister in reply to a parliamentary question, Finland's policy of neutrality excluded the participation of Finnish forces in joint military exercises with a foreign power.

The Finnish authorities played down the episode: after all, no formal proposal had been made. But the mystery lingers on. Why did Ustinov, at the time one of the most powerful men in the Kremlin, barge ahead without any advance soundings and in a manner bound to cause a leak to the press, thus putting himself in the embarrassing position of receiving a public snub?

An explanation may be found through an analysis of the general trend of Soviet policy in the late 1970s. In November 1976, 18 months before the Ustinov visit to Finland, Brezhnev visited Yugoslavia and presented Marshal Tito with a number of proposals designed to draw Yugoslavia into military cooperation with the Soviet Union. In this case, too, any competent student of international affairs could have told him his proposals would be rejected as incompatible with Yugoslavia's policy of nonalignment, and this is what in fact happened. In the following year, the Soviet Union began the deployment of SS20 missiles, with grave consequences for its relations with Western Europe. In 1978, while Ustinov was visiting Finland, Soviet garrisons were being established on three of the islands off the coast of Japan that Japan considers part of its own territory, an act that froze Soviet-Japanese relations for years to come. And a year later, at the end of 1979, the Soviet government ordered its forces to march into Afghanistan—a move that predictably caused profound damage to the political relations of the Soviet Union with both the West and leading Asian countries.

The pattern that emerges is revealing. Each of the actions I have mentioned had of course its local background and purpose. But they did have a common denominator: the primacy of military objectives over political considerations in Soviet decision making. In each case party leader Brezhnev appears to have listened to His Marshal's Voice. Fittingly, before his death, Brezhnev himself was elevated to the honorary rank of Soviet marshal, a gesture symbolizing his complete identification with the militarization of Soviet foreign policy.

In this light Ustinov's behavior in Helsinki in 1978 becomes understandable, as does Brezhnev's in Belgrade in 1976. Their purpose seems to have been to demonstrate their zeal in promoting the aspirations of the military leadership and, by doing so, to establish the line beyond which the goals of military policy could not profitably be pursued. In Finland, as in Yugoslavia, the Soviet suggestions of military cooperation, once rejected, were not mentioned again.

In Finnish-Soviet relations, 1978 marked the end of a period of roughly 10 years, during which Soviet policy seems to have been influenced to a greater extent than earlier by an ambition to draw Finland closer into the Soviet military system. At no time did the more assertive tendency toward Finland express itself in dramatic demands or overt pressure; it was more like an undercurrent flowing below the surface of official policy. The Ustinov affair, by bringing it into the open, put an end to it. Perhaps Brezhnev told his people, in the words of Czar Nicholas I, to leave Finland, a neighbor that had caused no trouble, alone. After the Ustinov visit, not even a hint of any desire for change in Finnish-Soviet relations was heard from Moscow.

## Finlandization

The ups and downs in Finnish-Soviet relations during the Cold War were reflected, sometimes as if by a distorting mirror, in changes in Western attitudes toward Finland. Having written off Finland after World War II as lost to communism, Western opinion at first regarded the Finnish claim of independence with the embarrassed disbelief with which families sometimes greet the return of a soldier who had been reported missing in action and presumed dead. Because the Finnish political leaders prudently played down any differences with the Soviet Union, their claim of independence had difficulty passing the decibel test often applied by Western commentators: the louder a country condemned the Soviet Union, the greater its independence.

As relations between East and West began to improve in the 1960s, it briefly appeared that both sides would finally overcome their misgivings about Finnish policy. In fact, however, détente was perceived on both sides as a threat to the cohesion within the respective alliances. Just as Moscow grew uneasy about the implications of Finnish neutrality for Eastern Europe, so did Western critics of détente fear the Finnish example might seduce West European nations into imagining that it would be possible to live in peace with the Soviet Union without the protection of a strong military alliance. In West Germany, Franz-Joseph Strauss, the Bavarian leader, launched a new political slogan in his campaign against Willy Brandt's Ostpolitik: Finlandization!

The term has been defined as a process by which a democratic nation living in the shadow of a militarily powerful totalitarian state gradually submits to the political domination of its neighbor and finally loses its internal freedom. This is of course just the opposite of what actually had happened to Finland, a country that by the end of the 1960s enjoyed greater freedom of action than anyone had imagined at the end of World War II. But Finlandization was not addressed to Finland itself. Not a description of historical reality, it was a warning of a fate worse than nuclear death awaiting the nations of Western Europe if they were foolish enough to trust Russians and lower their guard. Thus, for instance, the French writer Alain Minc devoted just one brief paragraph to Finland in his book entitled *Le Syndrome Finlandais* (1986).[11] The rest of the 235 pages were about the condition of Western Europe. By keeping silent, he wrote, Finland had been able to maintain its freedom because it could lean on the West, but Western Europe, if abandoned by the United States, would have no choice but to submit to Soviet blackmail. In his view, the hedonistic, overprotected societies of Western Europe, in spite of their great wealth and potential collective power, would simply lack the will to organize a defense on a scale that would maintain the balance of power in Europe. Put in this way, fear of Finlandization was yet another symptom of the inferiority complex that, like a bleeding ulcer, sapped the self-confidence of Western Europe in the 1970s.

Finland's "policy of silence" was believed to reveal a limitation of sovereignty, an abdication from the pursuit of the national interest. It was, of course, the very opposite: an expression of the "sacro egoismo" of the small nation, a rejection of the claims of ideological solidarity. By refraining from open criticism of Soviet violations of international law or human rights, the Finnish government sought to protect the human rights of Finnish citizens and defend the integrity of the Finnish state.

There are numerous historical precedents for such a policy. Henry Kissinger has described one in *A World Restored*, his study of the conditions in Europe after the French Revolution and Napoleon. A state defeated in war, Kissinger wrote, "may have to strive to save its national substance by adaptation to the victor. This is not necessarily a heroic policy, although in certain circumstances it may be the most heroic of all. To cooperate, without losing one's soul . . . what harder test of moral toughness exists?" This was the policy of Austria after 1809:

> It is a policy which places a peculiar strain on domestic principles of obligation for it can never be legitimized by its real motives. Its success depends on its appearance of sincerity, on the ability, as Metternich once said, of seeming the dupe without being it. . . . In such periods the knave and the hero, the traitor and the statesman are distinguished, not by their acts but by their motives. At what stage collaboration damages the national substance, at what point it becomes an excuse for an easy way out, these are questions that can be resolved only by people who have lived through the ordeal, not by abstract speculation. Collaboration can be carried out successfully only by a social organism of great cohesiveness and high morale. . . . [12]

This passage describes accurately the moral justification of Finland's policy after World War II, as well as the debilitating effect it had in the longer run. For the generation of Finns who had experienced the war, my generation, "seeming a dupe without being it" was a way to continue the defense of the country by other means. We knew without being told what kind of an adversary we faced: an evil empire. We understood instinctively that "whereof one cannot speak thereof one must be silent." But what we took for granted was not automatically transmitted to the next generation. As time went on, social cohesiveness and morale were eroded. Knaves and dupes among the politicians began to imitate President Kekkonen's back-channel diplomacy, letting Soviet representatives gain undue influence in Finnish domestic politics. In the 1970s a double standard in judging international events was adopted by many leading politicians. But the validity of a political concept is not nullified by human failings in its execution.

The self-censorship practiced by the Finnish media was singled out by Western critics as a particularly obnoxious feature of Finlandization, as if it were a Finnish invention unknown to other democracies. In fact, of course, self-censorship is practiced in every society where there is no official censor telling editors what may or may not be published. Freedom of the press makes every editor his own censor: he himself must decide what is "fit to print." The criteria vary from country to country and change with the times.

What happens when, for instance, an important state visit is in danger of being spoiled by the showing of a television program likely to offend the distinguished visitor? The prime minister calls the director of the television company and asks him to withdraw the program, and the director, being a patriotic man, agrees to do it. This is what happened in Britain when the king of Saudi Arabia was due to arrive and Prime Minister Margaret Thatcher discovered that the BBC was to broadcast a documentary about violations of human rights in the visitor's country. Had the Finnish prime minister taken similar action to placate a Soviet visitor it would have been held up by the world's press as an example of self-censorship.

In Finland it was taken for granted that a responsible editor would refrain from publishing material that might cause damage to the national interest. Until recently, the U.S. concept of the role of the media as a permanent adversary to authority was alien to Finland. The Finnish press was born in the nineteenth century when journalists had to find ways to get around the restrictions imposed by Russian censors, and the Finnish people learned to read between the lines. After liberation from Russian rule, self-censorship became a necessary element in the defense of national independence. During the 1930s and World War II, the Finnish press exercised great discretion in dealing with material related with Germany, and after the war it loyally supported President Paasikivi's efforts to gain the trust of the Soviet leadership. Editors took care not to cause damage to the policy of survival. This was surely the right thing to do. But in the 1970s the general decay of political morale affected the media as well, leading to excessive caution in editorial comments on Soviet policy, and in some cases even in reporting what went on in the Soviet Union. Today, all this is subject to a searching national debate: self-criticism has replaced self-censorship. The Finnish media have been "Americanized," for better and for worse.

## Appearance and Substance

After leaving the foreign service at the end of 1974, my books and newspaper articles criticized the "Finlandization" of Finnish political life, including self-censorship gone too far; at the same time, however, I defended Finnish policy against foreign critics. In my view the West, having failed to support Finland's democracy when it was threatened, had forfeited its moral right to criticize policies designed to ensure the survival of Finland as a democratic state. But more important, foreign critics tended to project a one-dimensional picture of Finland, failing to distinguish between appearance and substance.

One important aspect of Finland's policy during the Cold War almost totally ignored in the Finlandization debate was defense. Officially, the goal of Finland's security policy was to maintain neutrality in an East-West conflict in Europe, but a more down-to-earth, unspoken objective was to keep control over the country's territory at all times in Finnish hands.

Moscow had to be convinced that it was in the Soviet interest to leave the job of defending Finland to the Finns themselves. President Kekkonen's "preventive diplomacy" was one part of this effort of persuasion. The other part was to maintain a credible defense against a possible attempt by NATO forces to attack the Soviet Union through Finland. According to the Finnish interpretation of the 1948 treaty with the Soviet Union, military cooperation between the two parties was envisaged only in the event that Finnish neutrality had failed and Finnish territory had been attacked from the West. Even then responsibility for the defense of Finland would rest primarily with the Finns themselves, and Soviet assistance would be obtained only if needed.

Such explanations were usually brushed aside by Western critics as wishful thinking. Surely, it was said, the Soviet leaders would not let themselves be hobbled by legal niceties. In a critical situation they would do whatever they thought was necessary, regardless of what was written in the Finnish-Soviet treaty.

In any case, the West was more interested in what Finland might do in the event of an aggressive move by Soviet forces across Finnish territory into Sweden or Norway. The question was answered by President Kekkonen when, in 1965, he assured Finland's neighbors, Norway in particular, that Finland was not committed by treaty to join an aggression and would not permit another country to use Finnish territory for an aggressive purpose.

Yet doubt persisted, and in January 1983 General Bernard Rogers, then supreme commander of NATO forces in Europe, publicly questioned the willingness of the Finnish people to defend their country. His remarks revealed a disturbing ignorance, not just about Finland, but also about the nationalist undercurrents in countries under Soviet domination. It was assumed that the Poles or the Hungarians would obediently join Soviet forces in an aggression against the West, that the people of Czechoslovakia who for centuries had refrained from taking up arms against any nation would hurl themselves against their neighbors, or that East Germans would start killing West Germans in the name of an ideology that had lost its appeal.

The Soviets themselves had a more realistic view of the true nature of the Warsaw Pact. A prominent Soviet diplomat once said at a late-night session: "One American division plus one German division equals two NATO divisions; one Soviet division plus one Polish division equals zero Warsaw Pact divisions."

General Rogers' remark produced an indignant reaction in Finland. Unwittingly, the general had done the Finns a service. The debate his comment caused cleared the air. The doubts he had brought into the open were largely dispelled.

No one who knew Finland could doubt the will of the people to defend their country. In international polls conducted in several Western countries, young men of military age were asked two questions: Were they willing to defend their country should war break out, and did they believe in the ability of the armed forces to defend their country? On both questions the percentage of those answering yes was highest in Finland.

The response to questions of this kind is not a product of intellectual analysis: it is a gut reaction. The self-confidence of the young Finnish men grew out of the collective memory of Finland's success in defending itself in World War II. As Tony Judt points out in his essay on Europe *A Grand Illusion?*, Great Britain and Finland are the only two West European states to have emerged from World War II with a creditable military record of which to boast.[13]

The message of the polls was reinforced by the Finnish record of conscription. Throughout the Cold War era, more than 90 percent of the young men liable to military service actually completed their training each year. This was a higher percentage than in any other Western country. It provided Finland with trained reserves of more than half a million men. The army was, and still is, organized for what is called territorial defense, a polite term for guerrilla warfare. Because no one could seriously imagine that a NATO army might march from Norway through Sweden and Finland for an invasion of the Soviet Union, the implication of Finland's defense posture was obvious. It was to make clear that an attempt to impose Soviet "assistance" would meet with strong resistance. The Finnish army could not have stopped the Soviet forces at the border, but could have made the stay of uninvited guests most uncomfortable. This was the substance behind the politically correct appearance of "Friendship, Cooperation and Mutual Assistance" prescribed by the 1948 treaty.

In more concrete terms, the progress of the Finnish economy provided the real substance of the country's independence and constituted an effective line of defense against Soviet influence. Behind a smoke screen of political declarations designed to reassure the Soviet leaders, Finland was integrated, step by step, into the West European economic system.

At the end of the war, no one had imagined that Finland would catch up with Western Europe in less than three decades. To resettle the population of the lost province of Karelia, Parliament passed an act in 1945 that had created some 142,000 new holdings out of 2.8 million hectares of land, mostly by compulsory purchase. As a result, Finland was the only OECD country where the farm population increased after World War II. Close to half of the total population—47 percent—was still supported by farming and forestry, while the corresponding figure in Sweden was 20, in Denmark 24, and in Norway 27. The forest industry accounted for four-fifths of all exports. Finland was thus a one-crop country at the mercy of every shift in the international market for timber, pulp, and paper. The domestic market was too small to stimulate an industrial expansion, while access to external markets was restricted by the many trade barriers that divided postwar Europe.

The first opening was provided, surprisingly, by the war reparations demanded by the Soviet Union. At the Tehran Conference in 1943, Winston Churchill had tried to dissuade Stalin from asking heavy reparations from Finland, conceding, however, that "the Finns might cut down a few trees." But Stalin was not interested in trees, of which Russia itself had more than enough. He insisted that two-thirds of the goods to be delivered as reparations by Finland were to be ships, machinery, and other engineering products that Finland had never produced in sufficient quantities even for its own use, and only one-third in timber and paper products. To meet this demand, Finland had to double the capacity of its shipbuilding and engineering industries at an enforced pace, a task that was the economic equivalent of the war itself. A combination of public and private enterprise was used to build up the industrial capacity required.

Payment of the war indemnity brought about a change in the structure of industry and, as a consequence, in the pattern of foreign trade. Once the indemnity had been paid off in 1952, the Soviet Union began to buy from Finland the goods it had received free of charge until then. It looked at the time like a plot designed to absorb Finland by economic means, and that may indeed have been Moscow's intention; in the immediate postwar period, the political consequences of trade with the Soviet Union caused a great deal of uneasiness in Finland. In 1948–1950, and again in 1958, delays in trade talks in Moscow were used as political pressure. But as Finland's economy recovered, the roles were reversed. Instead of being drawn into the Soviet economic system, Finland exploited the backward Soviet market to its own advantage, just as had happened at the end of the nineteenth century.

Finnish exports of manufactured products were paid for by Soviet deliveries of oil and gas as well as some raw materials. Efforts to diversify Soviet exports to Finland had little success. The Soviet Union was simply incapable of producing goods that could successfully compete in the Finnish market. Finnish industry on its part acquired a protected corner of the vast Soviet market, notably about 20 percent of Soviet imports of ships. In general, Finnish exporters were also able to obtain high profit margins in their deals with the Soviets. Another advantage was that trade with the Soviet Union tended to shield Finland against world business cycles. The recessions caused by the rise in oil prices in the 1970s and 1980s had a reverse effect in Finland. As the value of Russia's oil exports to Finland increased, Finland could export more goods to the USSR. Thus trade with Russia was in effect countercyclical to Western trade.

While the Soviet share of Finland's total exports remained remarkably steady at an average 20 percent annually over four decades, the structure of Finland's economic relationship with Western Europe underwent a profound change. Having said no to the Marshall Plan, Finland was at first left behind Western Europe in economic development. Apart from missing out on direct dollar aid, Finland was excluded from the Organization for European Economic Cooperation (OEEC), the forerunner of today's OECD. Finnish policy had to employ a great deal of ingenuity to find roundabout ways of sharing in the continuing process of trade liberalization initiated by the OEEC. For instance, after the OEEC countries formed the European Payments Union to free currency transactions among them, in 1957 Finland founded its own payments union, the "Helsinki Club," to which all the OEEC countries adhered.

Finland faced a more complex problem when seven West European states, led by Britain in 1959, formed the European Free Trade Association (EFTA) to abolish customs duties on industrial goods and remove other barriers restricting trade between its member states. Because Britain at the time was Finland's biggest customer and the other members of the EFTA included some of Finland's main competitors in the British market, it was vitally important for Finland to join the group. But the Soviet Union was strongly opposed to both the EFTA and the European Economic Community (EEC), considering them hostile organizations that discriminated against Soviet exports.

President Kekkonen first promised the Soviet government that Finland would not join the EFTA, but then under intense domestic pressure negotiated a deal by which the EFTA joined Finland in a parallel organization, ensuring full Finnish access to the free trade area. He then went on the placate the Soviets with an agreement granting Soviet products access to the Finnish market on equal terms with EFTA products, a concession that had no practical importance but violated the principles of GATT, of which Finland was a member.

Kekkonen in effect double-crossed both sides. He got away with it because the British, with U.S. backing, were prepared to turn a blind eye to questionable Finnish maneuvers to ensure that Finland would stay within the Western orbit. At the same time Khrushchev, realizing that Kekkonen needed an EFTA deal to win the next election in 1962, wished to keep Finland under Kekkonen's leadership as a showcase of his policy of coexistence. The timing was lucky for Finland; in 1961, when Finland's agreement with EFTA was concluded, Khrushchev was still firmly in the saddle, able to keep his opponents at bay.

The association with EFTA, followed in 1972 by a free trade agreement on industrial goods with the EEC, transformed the Finnish economy. Industrialization was speeded up and exports were diversified, reducing dependence on the forest industry. By 1980, the farm population had dropped to 9 percent and kept going down.

Such radical structural change could not be carried out without pain. As forest labor was being mechanized, many small farmers lost their second income and had to find new employment. At this point the common labor market established in 1954 between the four Nordic countries—Denmark, Finland, Norway, and Sweden—proved its value. Finland was able to export its unemployment to its Western neighbors, mainly to Sweden. From 1966 to 1970, 125,000 Finns moved to Sweden to work, while only 42,000 returned to Finland. In the period 1976–1980, 66,000 emigrated to Sweden, and 31,000 returned. By the beginning of the 1980s, the Finnish economy had stabilized, and from 1980 to 1985 more people returned from Sweden to Finland than moved in the other direction.

The change in the structure of the Finnish economy also had political consequences, the most important of which was the decline of communism. The party had drawn much of its support from among poor farmers with small holdings in eastern and northern Finland who voted Communist as a protest against their conditions rather than from Marxist conviction. At the beginning of the 1970s, the Communist strongholds in the rural areas were being rapidly depopulated. The Scandinavian-style welfare system built up in the 1960s and 1970s removed much of the sense of insecurity and discontent that had fueled the Communist movement. In urban areas, the traditional working class subculture with its own newspapers and clubs was dissolved by the spread of middle class values and suburban living. Concepts like the class struggle and the dictatorship of the proletariat lost their relevance for all except a handful of believers. The number of seats held by the Communists and their allies in Parliament fell from 40 out of 200 in 1975 to 27 in 1984. In the elections of March 1987, for the first time two rival Communist parties put forward candidates. The result was a further drop in Communist strength. The "eurocommunist" party was reduced to 16 seats and the "dogmatists" to 4.

With growing prosperity, the gap between political appearances and the life of civil society in Finland became ever wider. While the politicians went on playing their word games with the Soviets, civil society went its own way. In many respects—lifestyles, consumer habits, fashions, television entertainment, holiday travel—Finland became indistinguishable from any other Western country. Older Finns complained that Finland had become "Americanized" to the detriment of traditional ties with Germany and France. Indeed, thanks to generous scholarship programs, the American influence in Finnish cultural life had become dominant. More than 90 percent of school children learn English as their first foreign language. German and French have been neglected; Russian-speakers are hard to find.

Political change lagged behind. Although his vitality was clearly ebbing, Kekkonen allowed himself in 1979 to be reelected for another six-year period. But in September 1981 he was incapacitated by senility and had to resign. New elections were set for January 1982. The political establishment was deeply worried: who could replace the irreplaceable? Some politicians were inclined to look to Moscow for guidance, and Moscow did have its favorite candidate. But the voters did not want another Kekkonen. Mauno Koivisto, the candidate of the Social Democratic Party, received strong support across party lines. He won on character rather than on policy issues.

Moscow was resigned to the change. Once again, the timing was right. The Soviet Union was on the defensive. The invasion of Afghanistan had gone wrong, and President Ronald Reagan's policy of rearmament presented an economic and technological challenge the Soviet system was unable to meet. Stagnation was a word more frequently used to describe the Soviet condition. The best Moscow could hope for was to keep relations with Finland on a stable course. This suited Finland well. Stagnation in the Soviet Union meant peace and prosperity for Finland.

## The Other Neighbor

Preoccupation with Finnish-Soviet relations tended to obscure the profound importance of Sweden for developments in Finland. Unlike the politically motivated Soviet effort, the influence of Sweden was, and still is, part of the interaction between two open societies intertwined by innumerable ties and interests. Two peoples divorced after a long marriage and pulled apart by forces beyond their control, Finns and Swedes have a complex relationship of shared values and sharply different experiences. They are strongly bound by their common heritage of law, religion, and culture;

countless family ties; their growing economic interdependence; the use of Swedish as the language of communication between Finns and Swedes; and the current presence of a large Finnish-speaking minority in Sweden. Yet the geopolitical divide between Finland and Sweden, and the two centuries of separation caused by it, have left deep marks on both countries.

At the end of World War II, a Finn visiting Sweden felt uncomfortable and resentful like an impoverished and shabby country cousin invited into the house of a rich and sophisticated relative, yet at the same time looked down on his host with the peculiar sense of superiority that those who have suffered and survived feel toward their more fortunate neighbors. In the Finnish view, Sweden had let Finland down and had enriched itself while Finland fought against the common enemy. In the crucial weeks before the Winter War, the slogan "Finland's cause is ours" had had a strong appeal in Sweden, and manifestations of solidarity and support had created the impression that Sweden would come to the aid of Finland. But in confidential talks between the two governments, it had been made quite clear that Sweden would not go to war if Finland were attacked. In terms of international law, Sweden was not neutral during the Winter War; it allowed a force of 8,000 volunteers to fight on the eastern front and supplied Finland with material assistance. But this kind of support, although valuable, weighed little on the emotional scales.

The common Finnish belief was that Finland's successful resistance saved Sweden too. Had Finland been conquered by the Soviet Union in 1940, Sweden could hardly have been able to maintain its neutrality in 1941, not because of any Soviet intention to advance further, but because Hitler would have needed Sweden, instead of Finland, as a staging area for his invasion of the Soviet Union.

After the war, Swedish policy was to support Finland's independence, but in a tactful manner, so as not to add to Finland's difficulties in dealing with the Soviet Union. When Americans claimed that it was immoral for Sweden not to join the common defense of the free world, Swedes played their "Finnish card": by staying neutral Sweden claimed to help Finland to keep the Soviets out. The assumption was that, had Sweden joined NATO, the Soviet Union would have moved its military positions into Finland. Were the Soviet Union to force Finland into closer military cooperation, it was further implied, Sweden would reconsider its policy of neutrality. Either way, we shall never know. The "Finnish card" was actually more of an alibi for Swedish neutrality than a credible deterrent to any possible Soviet move against Finland.

As Finland's position stabilized and Finnish neutrality became more widely accepted, it became customary to describe Finnish and Swedish foreign policies as parallel or even identical. But the geopolitical divide, though blurred, was not erased. In practice, Sweden's policy of neutrality was different from Finland's. A malicious Finnish diplomat once defined the difference by saying that Finland tried to maintain good relations with both sides in the Cold War, while Sweden insulted both evenhandedly. There is some truth in this. Although Finland kept a low profile on issues dividing the Soviet Union and the West, Sweden did not hesitate to criticize both sides. The attacks of the Swedish government against U.S. policy in Vietnam became so harsh that Washington withdrew the U.S. ambassador from Stockholm for several years. In all fairness it should be pointed out that Sweden also condemned the Soviet occupation of Czechoslovakia more severely than did other Western governments, including the United States.

For Finland this Swedish activism was at times inconvenient. Soviet diplomats would ask why did not Finland "struggle for the cause of peace" as energetically as did Sweden. But points were gained in Washington. Henry Kissinger never stopped praising Finland's restraint.

These were mere wrinkles on the surface of things. The real impact Sweden had on Finnish life in the 1960s and 1970s was in the domain of social policy. To catch up with Sweden became a national goal in the pursuit of which all Finns could unite their efforts. But it meant catching up with Sweden not only in creating wealth but also in spending it. In the latter half of the 1960s, a rapid expansion of the public sector was undertaken in Finland under the leadership of the Social Democratic Party. It used to be said, only half in jest, that Swedish social legislation was translated unchanged into Finnish and enacted by Parliament. The growth of public spending went on through the 1970s in tandem with that in Sweden, reaching 40 percent of GDP in 1979. At that point, however, the trend was halted in Finland, again under the leadership of the Social Democrats, while in Sweden it went on to reach 60 percent of GDP. The Finnish party made its U-turn in time, a quarter-century before Tony Blair.

There is in fact a fundamental difference between the Social

Democratic parties in Finland and Sweden, in spite of the close ties existing between them. Except for short intervals, the Swedish Social Democrats have been in power for more than 60 years. They are firmly entrenched in the labor unions as well as in the central administration and local government. As a result they have acquired a strong sense of political self-sufficiency, combining practical competence in the running of the machinery of state with an ideological commitment to the concept of democratic socialism or socialist democracy—the "third way." The Finnish party has never won more than 28 percent of the votes in parliamentary elections after World War II and has had to fight a tough struggle against the Communists on the left. The Finnish Social Democrats have always had to cooperate with other parties on equal terms, which has ensured victory of pragmatism over ideology.

There were other important differences between the two countries. Sweden was way ahead of Finland in the internationalization of industry and business. The industrial boom in the 1960s brought a flood of foreign workers into the country. Sweden was wide open to immigration: today, one eighth of the Swedish population, more than a million people, are either immigrants or children of immigrants. In contrast, Finland maintains the restrictive attitude to immigration it developed in the nineteenth century. Finland remains closed, like a hedgehog.

As a result, Finland and Sweden have grown apart in many respects. The Swedes pride themselves on being number one in the world in social liberalism on issues like abortion, women's rights, and attitudes toward sexual minorities. Sweden has also been in the vanguard in promoting environmental protection, both nationally and internationally. Finnish society has been, and still is, more conservative, although influenced by the Swedish example.

The Swedish paradox of social utopianism combined with hardheaded realism in business and industry was personified in Olof Palme, leader of the Social Democratic Party and prime minister, 1969–1976 and 1982–1986. I got to know him in the late 1950s, when he was Prime Minister Tage Erlander's principal assistant. Erlander was rather unique among politicians; by stepping down before he had to, he gave Palme a chance. Thus Palme was prime minister when I was appointed ambassador to Stockholm in 1972.

Palme, too, was unique among the common run of politicians in the Scandinavian countries, but in a different sense. He had grown up in an upper-middle-class professional family and had received a cosmopolitan education. As a result, he was fluent in English, German, and French and had an intense interest in international affairs. In contrast to his more down-to-earth colleagues in the party leadership, Palme had a passionate commitment to socialist ideology and, in spite of his background, achieved a dominant position in the Social Democratic movement, while reviled by conservatives as a traitor to his class.

In private conversation, I found Palme a brilliant and realistic analyst of politics—international affairs in particular. But when he rose to make a speech in Parliament or at a political meeting, he was transformed into a demagogue. His love of polemics often led him to excesses—when, for instance, he compared U.S. policy in Vietnam to Nazi atrocities, words that denied him an invitation to Washington. He was labeled anti-American, but in fact his political style was American rather than Scandinavian. He had spent a year as a student in the United States, and his campaign against the Vietnam War used arguments and slogans imported from U.S. campuses.

A traditional policy of neutrality did not satisfy Palme. His ambition was to make his mark on the world as champion of universal human rights and social justice in international relations: the third way transposed onto the world scene. But when it came to Sweden's national security or vital economic interests, Palme was no naive dove. As we now know, under his leadership Sweden secretly cooperated with NATO to make sure the country would be prepared to receive military assistance in the event of a Soviet aggression.

Like Urho Kekkonen in Finland, Palme justified his obvious love of power on idealistic grounds: He needed power to accomplish his mission. But to stay in power he had to compromise his ideological convictions. As a result he was condemned by his critics twice: first, because he was a utopian, then because he was an opportunist.

In his personal life, Palme was a paragon of modesty, almost ascetic. I once bumped into him at Stockholm airport standing patiently in a long line of passengers waiting to be checked in. He insisted on leading a normal private life with his wife and family. No security men followed him around: who would need them in peaceful Stockholm. And so, on February 28, 1986, walking home with his wife from a movie in the center of the city, Olof Palme was shot dead, and the murderer escaped into the night. This inexplicable crime adds one more to a series of unsolved mysteries in Swedish history: Who killed Charles XII? Was the death of Ivar Kreuger the "match king" really suicide? What is the truth about Raoul Wallenberg's death? How did Dag Hammarskjöld die? The murder of Palme is still being investigated, but by now the trail is cold.

Five months after the murder, former president Urho Kekkonen died in retirement. The two funerals illustrated the deep gulf that separates Finland and Sweden.

The burial of Olof Palme was organized by the Social Democratic Party, not by the Swedish state. The City Hall of Stockholm, where the ceremony was held, and the entire route of the funeral procession, were drenched in the color red—the flags of the labor movement. The main funeral oration was held by the new party leader Ingvar Carlsson, and the civil burial act was performed by the former party secretary, Foreign Minister Sten Andersson. The king of Sweden, seated in the far end of the row of invited guests, had to wait his turn to speak as number three. The emblem of the United Nations formed the background to the coffin, and the UN flag was carried along two red party flags at the head of the procession, with one lonely blue-and-yellow Swedish flag at their side. The UN secretary-general was one of the speakers, followed by the prime minister of India, Rajiv Gandhi, and by the chairman of the Socialist International, Willy Brandt of Germany. The symbolism was obvious: The murdered prime minister was accompanied to his grave by the party, the Socialist International, the United Nations, and the Third World. The kingdom of Sweden, the nation, the state, had a secondary role.

Urho Kekkonen too had been in many ways a radical who had defied convention, not a church-going man. But as a former president, he was buried with all the traditional honors. The funeral service was held in the Lutheran Cathedral of Helsinki, with the archbishop officiating. The funeral oration was given by the president of the republic, and the coffin was carried by eight bemedaled generals. Here, too, the message was clear: The republic, the nation, the fatherland will live on.

# 4

# Integration

In 1991, as in 1917, the Eastern colossus fell apart. Did we in Finland see this coming? Finns were widely believed to have the key to what Winston Churchill once called the "riddle wrapped in a mystery inside an enigma." Typically, former German chancellor Helmut Schmidt wrote in his 1990 memoirs that the Finns were well ahead of Western Europe in their knowledge of what was going on in their Eastern neighbor. As evidence he singled out an analysis of the state of the Soviet Union I had written in 1984.[1] It would be gratifying now to quote from my text passages predicting the decline and fall of the Soviet empire. But I cannot find even a hint of this. I described the Soviet Union as a state in stagnation, determined to maintain the status quo. I suspect Helmut Schmidt liked my analysis because it coincided with his own at the time. In a lecture in Helsinki in 1988, he said that German unification was inevitable—in 50 years. For people living now, 50 years is a synonym for never.

None of us diplomats, scholars, journalists, or spies can claim to have foreseen the sudden breakdown of Soviet power. We counted the missiles and warheads without due regard to the economic and social context of the Soviet Union's military might; we watched the goings on in the Kremlin, ignoring the cracks at the base of the Soviet power structure.

A candid appraisal of the reasons for this massive failure of intelligence could teach us something for next time. One reason, or perhaps excuse, is that while in theory analysis is an independent function, in practice research and intelligence merge into the policymaking process. Assessments are made within the framework of established concepts, or paradigms, and as time passes, powerful interests build up in defense of continuity. To challenge established concepts is to risk being dismissed as a crank or a utopist.

As an ethnographer during the Soviet period, Estonia's president Lennart Meri had crisscrossed the vast interior of Russia studying the surviving remnants of Finno-Ugric communities. In a 1996 interview, he said he had understood in the early 1980s what "40,000 well paid American sovietologists had failed to grasp"—that the Soviet system was piling debt upon debt in a vicious circle that was bound to lead to catastrophe. Had the Finns understood? he was asked. In reply, he told of his first visit to Finland in 1974. The first thing he saw from his hotel window was graffiti sprayed on the wall opposite proclaiming: "The Yanks out of Angola!" No, Meri said, the Finns had not understood either.[2]

His point was that Western intellectuals had refused to recognize the fact that the Soviet Union was a vast colonial power doomed to share the fate of all such empires. There is some truth in this. American opinion had been slow to realize that the ideological worldview fostered by the Cold War was a misleading description of reality. Washington continued to believe in the existence of a China-Soviet bloc long after the differences between the national interests of the Soviet Union and China had caused an irrevocable rift between them. Inspired by their own ideology of One World, Americans overrated the strength of the opposing ideology of communism. Indeed, President George Bush went to great lengths to help Mikhail Gorbachev to resist the rising tide of nationalism within the Soviet Union. West Germans, too, made the mistake of believing that East Germany, the German Democratic Republic (GDR), was the strongest bastion of Soviet power in Europe. I wrote in December 1988 that the weakening of the Communist ideology would have fatal consequences for the GDR: "Poland will always be Poland, Hungary will be Hungary, regardless of the system of government in those countries. But the DDR [GDR] will lose the very reason of its existence if it ceases to be socialist."[3] It was not an accident that the unraveling of the Soviet outer empire started with the spontaneous mass exodus of the citizens of the GDR.

There was one man who did predict the fall of the Soviet Union—President Ronald Reagan. In his address to both houses of the British Parliament in 1982, he confidently declared that the end of the Soviet state was in sight: "The Communist system will be remembered as a brief parenthesis in human history." We the experts passed this over with an ironical smile: What could a Californian actor know about such things? But of course Reagan's prediction was not based on superior knowledge: it was an expression of faith.

U.S. President Reagan was also in the position of being able to help his prediction come true. Obviously, Reagan's policy of rearmament was not the only factor that brought the Soviet empire to a fall. I do believe, however, that it hastened the end. I could sense its effect on the Soviet representatives I used to meet in Helsinki in the 1980s. Some were simply scared: Do you believe he really means what he says? Others defiant: We will match every new weapon the Americans produce, cost what it may. But all had become very cautious. They sensed the change in "the correlation of forces."

The reason why we in Finland nevertheless failed to see what was coming was simple. The Finnish people "had never had it so good" as in the time of Soviet stagnation. Relations with Moscow were stable and predictable; business was booming. In internal politics, a wide-ranging consensus had emerged across the dividing line between Right and Left. Militant communism had dwindled to a fringe group. International bankers awarded the country with a triple-A rating for creditworthiness. Finns no longer felt themselves to be menaced by the East and let down by the West, walking a tightrope without a safety net. Rather, Dag Hammarskjöld's dictum that to be born in Scandinavia is like receiving a winning ticket in life's lottery had been adopted by Finns as their new national motto. In an opinion poll conducted in the mid-1980s, more than eight out of ten interviewed agreed with the statement that it was "a good fortune and privilege" to be a Finn. People satisfied with things as they are do not expect or predict change, because they do not believe that change could be for the better.

Of course Mikhail Gorbachev's perestroika raised great hopes in Finland as everywhere else in the Western world, but Finns on the whole were less inclined to believe that the Soviet system could actually be reformed. The skeptics were right, but they were wrong about the consequences of Gorbachev's failure. They took for granted that it would bring the hardliners back into power. The first news, on August 19, 1991, of the attempted coup d'état in Moscow was received by many Finns with the words: I told you so. Some may still today insist that sooner or later Russia will "return to normal"—to authoritarian rule.

In contrast, the Estonians across the Gulf of Finland expected and predicted the collapse of the Soviet Union, because for them the conditions they lived in were intolerable. While Finland, like the West in general, backed Gorbachev on the ground that any alternative was likely to be worse, the Estonians and the other Baltic peoples had no faith in perestroika and placed their bets on Boris Yeltsin, whom the West regarded as a troublemaker. President Mauno Koivisto, like George Bush, advised the Baltic leaders not to rock the boat and to make the best of the advantages offered by Gorbachev's reforms, but the Balts were determined to seize the opportunity to restore the independence of their countries.

We now know that the Balts were right: Boris Yeltsin, like Samson, brought down the whole edifice of the Soviet empire on Gorbachev's head, releasing the Baltic peoples into freedom. They were right partly because they had inside knowledge of the rotten state of the Soviet Union. But the difference between Western and Baltic perceptions had deeper roots. Western governments misjudged the Soviet situation because they were comfortable with the status quo; the possibility of revolutionary change was too disturbing to contemplate. As former U.S. ambassador to Moscow Jack Matlock has pointed out, U.S. policy was to put the ideological goal of promoting democracy in the Soviet Union ahead of the liberation of the "captive nations." But nationalism was the stronger force.[4] The Baltic peoples, too, wanted democracy, but they were convinced that only independence could enable them to create a genuine democratic system. "Democracy was born with the sense of nationality: The two are inherently linked."[5]

Many Finns were offended by President Koivisto's cold-blooded attitude to the Baltic independence movements. In fact he was entirely in line with Western policy, only less hypocritical in expressing it. He later explained he wanted to avoid raising among the Baltic peoples false hopes of Western support against the possible use of force by the Soviets. He had not forgotten the lesson of Hungary in 1956.

As Soviet power waned, Finland began to edge toward full participation in Western institutions, but gingerly, like a hunter who has shot a bear but is not quite sure the beast is dead. In January 1986 Finland finally became a full member of the European

Free Trade Association, and in spring 1989 Finland joined the Council of Europe. In September 1990 the Finnish government unilaterally abrogated the clauses in the 1947 peace treaty that imposed limitations on Finland's armed forces and declared that the references to Germany as a potential enemy in the Finnish-Soviet treaty of 1948 had lost their validity. But it waited until October 1991 before renegotiating the treaty itself, and the new version, shorn of any references to possible military cooperation, remained unsigned when the Soviet Union ceased to exist, taking the old treaty with it into the grave.

Before this, Finland's 40-year pursuit of international recognition for its neutrality had finally reached its goal. In May 1988 President Reagan stopped over in Helsinki on his way to Moscow and declared: "America respects Finland's neutrality. We support Finland's independence." Five months later Mikhail Gorbachev visited Finland and recognized Finnish neutrality without reservations, promising to respect it. But very soon Finland found itself in the position of a suitor who had had to wait for his bride for so long that he was too old to consummate the marriage. Neutrality as practiced in the Cold War was rendered obsolete by the fast pace of change in Europe—integration in the West and disintegration in the East.

## Finland Joins the Union

The break-up of the Soviet empire was greeted in Finland with profound relief, yet tempered by cautionary warnings not to forget that Russia would always remain a great power. President Boris Yeltsin's first visit to Finland in 1991 was replete with symbols of a new beginning between the two countries. He paid his respects to the memorial for the Finnish soldiers killed defending their country against the Soviet invasion, a gesture none of the Soviet leaders, not even Gorbachev, had made. The Russian president also called the Finnish-Soviet treaty of 1948 an "unjust document" and apologized for Soviet interventions in Finland's domestic affairs. He promised to conduct relations with Finland without "the hypocrisy and pretense" of the Soviet era. And Patriarch Aleksei, the head of the Russian orthodox church, went further: he asked for forgiveness for the Soviet invasion of Finland in 1939.

Russia's apparent willingness to make amends revived among

some Finns the long-dormant hope that Moscow might agree to return the land the Soviets had seized in the war. The organization representing the Karelians who had lost their homes petitioned the government to raise the issue with the Russians. This was not done. The government knew that Russia was as opposed to a revision of frontiers as had been the Soviet Union, nor would a Finnish claim receive support from the West. Germany in particular was anxious to set aside territorial issues.

There were also more down-to-earth reasons for not seeking a return of Karelia. The territory is in miserable shape. In 1994, I went along with a group of fellow veterans on a visit to the places where we fought in 1941–1944. It was a depressing experience: everywhere neglect and decay, poverty, and backwardness. An immense effort of reconstruction would be required to make the area once again habitable for Finns. No economic incentive for such an undertaking exists. Finland needs no more farmland, and the forest resources of Karelia are already exploited by Finnish industry across the border. An additional burden would be the present population of about 300,000, mainly from Russia, Belarus, and Ukraine. For most of them, Karelia is now their home; they could not be driven away in an act of ethnic cleansing.

Altogether, the case against claiming the lost territory is over-whelming, and opinion polls indicate that the great majority of Finnish people agree with it, which I believe is a victory of common sense over the nostalgic and romantic notion that it is the nation's duty to reclaim every inch of soil it has once possessed. Blood comes before soil. The Karelians had proved this in 1944 by leaving their land rather than live under Soviet rule. Had a significant number of them stayed, the territorial issue would have been a running sore in Finnish-Soviet relations, and the demand for a revision of frontiers could not have been resisted by any Finnish government.

In spite of Finnish restraint, however, the status quo could not be maintained. In the beginning of 1990, Moscow moved to free foreign trade, which ended the bilateral trading system with Finland. As a result, trade with Russia declined from more than 20 percent of Finland's external trade in the 1980s to less than 3 percent in 1992, and the number of workers supported by exports to the Soviet Union plunged from 230,000 in 1981 to fewer than 50,000 in 1992. The industrial enterprises grown soft after 40 years of "managed trade" with the Soviet Union were slow to respond. An important part of Finland's industry had been molded by inefficient cost structures, particularly with regard to staffing levels, and a general lack of competitiveness by Western standards.

The collapse of trade with Russia coincided with a recession in Finland's western export markets. The liberalization of capital movements initiated in 1986 led to excessive lending by the banks and financial speculation. The bubble burst in the beginning of the 1990s. The banking system had to be bailed out by the government. The Finnish currency, the markka, which had been tied to the European exchange rate mechanism in June 1991, had to be devalued less than six months later, and in September 1992 speculators forced the Bank of Finland to let the markka float, which caused a 17 percent fall in value against the deutsche mark. Finland's GDP dropped by almost 15 percent, a contraction unprecedented in an OECD country, and the jobless rate reached 20 percent in 1993.

In the midst of the worst slump since the early 1930s, Finland faced a new challenge from Western Europe. The European Community (soon to become the European Union) under the leadership of the president of the European Commission, Jacques Delors, was engaged in establishing a single market, with freedom of movement for goods, capital, services, and labor. The EFTA-countries (Austria, Finland, Norway, Sweden, and Switzerland) were all heavily dependent in their foreign trade on the European Community: they were determined to make sure their enterprises would have access to the single market. In response, Jacques Delors proposed in January 1989 the creation of a European Economic Area (EEA), comprising both the European Community and the EFTA, designed to make the latter part of the single market without membership in the Community itself. This was a defensive move by Delors, who wished to protect the political cohesion of the EC by keeping the neutral countries out.

The Delors model—economic access without political commitment—seemed tailor-made for Finland. The exclusion of agriculture from the EEA was also a great relief from the Finnish point of view. The EEA negotiations started in the beginning of 1990 and were completed in October 1991, but when Switzerland withdrew, a new round of negotiations was needed, and the treaty was not signed until in March 1993. But by that time the EFTA front had crumbled. The first country to defect was Austria, which announced at the end of 1989 that it would seek full membership in the European Community; in October 1990 the Swedish government followed suit: neutrality was no longer considered an obstacle to EC membership.

In Finland every politician hurried to declare that the Swedish decision would have absolutely no effect on Finnish policy. But everyone understood that once Sweden had moved, Finland could not remain outside. The question was no longer whether or not Finland would apply; it was how and when the decision would be reached.

The problem was that in Finland, as elsewhere in Europe, the issues raised by deepening integration cut across traditional party lines, throwing the parliamentary system out of gear. Parliaments revolve around the Right-Left axis, which is losing its relevance, while the more pressing issues of integration are fought over across a different divide.

In the Finnish case, the election in March 1991 had brought into power a coalition consisting of the Center Party (formally the Agrarian Party) and the Conservative Party, reinforced by a couple of smaller groups, while the Social Democrats remained in opposition. This right-of-center coalition could agree on economic and social policies, but was split on the European Community. The Center Party, which traditionally represents the farming community and the less-developed regions of eastern and northern Finland, was against seeking membership, while the Conservatives were for it, as was the main opposition party, the Social Democrats.

To disentangle the crossed wires took some time. The Finnish leaders also kept looking over their shoulders at the growing tension within the Soviet Union. The failure of the coup in August 1991 was a turning point. Soon after, President Koivisto, who had held his cards close to his chest, ordered the government to make a comprehensive study of a possible membership in the EC, and in January 1992 he made his own view known. In a simple but telling phrase, the president said that it would be in the Finnish interest to "be represented at the table where decisions are made." Backed by the president, Prime Minister Esko Aho, leader of the Center Party, was able to persuade enough members of his own party to vote in Parliament in favor of an application to join the EU. It helped of course that with the votes of the Social Democrats, a majority for joining was in any case assured. Finally, 133 out of 200 members voted in favor of applying for membership.

Brussels began talks with Austria, Finland, and Sweden in February 1993, and with Norway a couple of months later; talks were completed in March 1994. In the meantime the European Community had adopted the Maastricht Treaty and turned itself into the European Union. Compared with the seven years' work needed to bring Spain, Portugal, and Greece into the EU, the accession talks with the Nordic countries and Austria were relatively painless. The Maastricht Treaty had to be signed by the applicant countries without reservation, and economic issues had largely been resolved in the talks on the European Economic Area. Furthermore, all the applicants had a national income higher than the EU average and were welcomed as net contributors to the common budget. In this respect, the next round of enlargement will be quite different: the former Communist countries will all need heavy subsidies from existing member states.

In the case of Finland, the main problem in the accession negotiation was agriculture, a branch of the economy that at the time accounted for less than 3 percent of GDP and employed 7 percent of the total labor force. Yet in Finland, as in France, the importance of farming cannot be measured by percentage counts. The rural landscape was the original inspiration of patriotism as extolled by poets and artists in the nineteenth century. It is still an essential element in the Finnish self-image. A majority of the urban population is only one or two generations removed from the farms, and more than 400,000 vacation homes, ranging from well-appointed villas to primitive log cabins or cottages, attest to the Finnish passion for country life.

More than nostalgia was involved in the Brussels talks. Because more than 60 percent of Finland's forests are owned and cared for by the farmers, there was a direct link to the interests of the powerful forest industry. Another dimension was national defense. If large parts of eastern and northern Finland were to be depopulated, the present system of territorial defense could be undermined.

The negotiations on agriculture thus touched the fundamental dilemma inherent in the process of integration: How to reconcile economic and commercial rationality with the immaterial values and interests embedded in the traditional structures of the society?

Rationality clearly required a drastic reduction in Finnish agriculture. Two land reforms, the first in the early 1920s and the second as part of the resettlement of the Karelians, had created a large number of farms too small to remain viable. The northern climate makes average production costs considerably higher in Finland than in countries like Denmark or Holland. The need for rationalization had therefore been evident for some time. In Brussels, the issue was at what pace rationalization would be carried out, and how subsidies were to be divided between the EU and Finland itself. Naturally, the Finnish farmers were dissatisfied with the outcome. Objectively, however, the Finnish negotiators succeeded fairly well. But the future trend is inevitable: in 1994 the number of farms was 121,000, in 1996 it had dropped to 92,000, and it is expected to level at 65,000. The remaining farms will be bigger and presumably more profitable.

After the conclusion of the accession treaty with the European Union governments, the next step for Finland and the other applicants was to consult their electorates by way of referendums. The Finnish people were not accustomed to such a procedure. The last and only time a referendum had been held in Finland was in 1931, when the issue was whether to continue U.S.-style prohibition. On this subject no one could question the expert knowledge of the Finnish people, and they duly made the right decision: prohibition was ended. But joining the European Union was a complex issue on which few citizens could claim to be well informed; surely it was best left to the elected representatives of the people to be decided in Parliament. Yet the Finnish government passed the buck to the voters. A referendum was held on October 16, 1994.

The reason was partly that the other applicant countries— Austria, Norway and Sweden—had decided to submit the issue to referendums, and Finnish politicians had to show equal trust in the judgment of the people. There was, however, another, less idealistic motive for their decision. A vote in Parliament would have split every party—a nightmare for the party managers. The referendum was a way out. Although it was consultative and thus reserved the final decision for Parliament, all the parties committed themselves in advance to respect its outcome. This enabled some members of Parliament to have their cake and eat it too—to oppose membership and then to vote for it.

The use of referendums is defended on the ground that it provides democratic legitimacy to Union decisions, bridging the gap between Brussels and the peoples. Even in Britain, the motherland of the parliamentary system, both major parties have committed themselves to holding a referendum on Economic and Monetary Union (EMU), thus tacitly admitting that the traditional party system is unable to cope with the issue.

Allowing the people to decide by direct vote whether they

wish their country to join the European Union, or such projects as EMU, may seem an enhanced form of democratic decision making, but it has serious drawbacks. The Finnish referendum is a case in point. Opposition to EU membership brought together a bizarre coalition. Right-wing nationalists and former Communists stood side by side in defense of sovereignty; conservative farmers joined liberal intellectuals in attacking the Union as too market-oriented; feminists believed the status of women would suffer from association with countries like Spain or Greece; environmentalists were convinced Finnish standards were higher than those in most EU countries; and Lutheran fundamentalists regarded Brussels as an annex to the Vatican. The only thing they all shared was a passionate opposition to Finland's entry into the European Union. The referendum gave them the opportunity to vote no without having to take responsibility for the consequences of their action. To believe that by keeping Finland outside of the Union everything would remain as it had been was of course an illusion. Had the opposition succeeded, Finland would have been left in limbo, without a coherent alternative policy on how to deal with the relentless march of integration in Europe. If a decision to reject membership had been taken in Parliament, the opposition would have had to form a new government and provide such an alternative.

Referendums are also more unpredictable than parliamentary elections. Their outcome is often influenced by factors unrelated to the issue at hand. To call a referendum is always a gamble, like placing your bet on rouge ou noir. This is especially true when voters are asked to decide whether or not to adopt a complex document like the Maastricht Treaty. Multilateral agreements usually contain clauses that, by the tacit consent of all parties, can be interpreted in different ways. Such ambiguity is part of international life, but in a referendum it is yes or no without qualifications. The fate of the Maastricht Treaty in Denmark is a case in point. It was first rejected by the Danish people, then after cosmetic changes accepted in a second round.

Although the Danes voted for or against "ever closer union" as defined in the Maastricht Treaty, the Finnish voters had other things on their minds. As opinion surveys indicate, for many the referendum was a choice between two evils. Among those who voted yes to membership, there was little enthusiasm for the Union as an institution, yet the alternative of staying outside seemed worse. It would have left Finland isolated, next door to a former superpower in a state of internal turmoil. The majority of 57 percent who said yes to Union membership wished to affirm Finland's Western identity and thereby strengthen the country's security. The strongest supporters of joining were the younger, better educated people living in urban areas—those in tune with the change of the times.

In contrast, the Norwegians, sheltered by NATO, could take it for granted that their country was part of the West; they could afford to say no to the European Union to assert their separate identity. In Sweden, many voters on the Left opposed EU membership on the ground that it might endanger the Swedish social model, which they considered superior to anything existing on the continent. To each of the three Nordic countries, "Europe" meant, and still means, something different. In each case, attitudes have been shaped by geography and historical experience, not abstract concepts.

The Finnish preoccupation with security was underlined by President Mauno Koivisto in a memoir written after Finland's entry into the European Union. He wrote that his decision to advocate membership had been based primarily on considerations of national security, rather than economic interest, but he had refrained from saying so publicly before Finland had actually been accepted as a member. Had something gone wrong and Finland's bid to enter the Union failed, it could have been said that the country was less secure than before. Some critics accused him of misleading the voters by keeping quiet about his motives, but I would call it an example of statesmanship.

## Toward a Single Currency

Once inside, Finland has to face the question of what is meant by "ever closer union." A cliché often repeated in the current debate is that powerful transnational forces fueled by technological advances have rendered the nation-state obsolete. Because no government is able to contain these forces by purely national means, the European Union could be described as an attempt by its member states to regain collectively part of the sovereignty each individually has had to yield to the market. Accordingly, it is argued that the Union must now proceed from the single market to EMU with a single currency and a common central bank. This transition in turn will make it necessary to form a stabilization pact to ensure that none of the members of EMU strays from the narrow path prescribed by the need to keep the single currency, the euro, stable and strong.

The economic arguments advanced for the EMU project are well known: The single market will not work properly without a single currency, the end of currency fluctuations will ensure a stable environment for investments and steady growth, and a single currency is needed to free Europe from its dependence on the ups and downs of the U.S. dollar and the turns and twists of U.S. economic policy. In opposition, many economists argue that the European Union has not yet reached the degree of economic convergence necessary for the operation of a single currency. The single market, they point out, is flawed because the freedom of movement for labor is largely theoretical in a culturally divided Europe.

If a referendum on EMU were to be carried out among the world's economists, a majority would probably vote no. U.S. economists, in particular, have voiced criticism of the EMU project, perhaps, one suspects, because of a subconscious desire to prevent the emergence of a rival to the almighty dollar.

Supporters of EMU respond by shifting the goalposts. It is not the economy after all, they say: EMU is at heart a political or, more precisely, an ideological project. Behind it lurk the demons of the past. Both Germans and French are driven by their nightmares. The single currency is designed to nail down irreversibly the German commitment to European unity. Now is the last moment to institutionalize German power within the European Union, for the successors to Chancellor Helmut Kohl may not be able, or willing, to stem the flood of "D-mark nationalism"—a phrase used by former chancellor Helmut Schmidt.

It was in this spirit that the leaders of the European Union acted in Maastricht in 1991. Trusting neither each other nor themselves, they straitjacketed their governments to rigid convergence criteria and an immutable timetable to ensure that all would be legally obligated to stick to a strict financial diet so as to be fit for monetary union in 1999. This has worked insofar as it has enabled governments to invoke the higher authority of the Maastricht Treaty to justify unpopular budget cuts they would have had to make anyway, EMU or no EMU, to reduce public debt, and bring down inflation and interest rates.

For a small country like Finland, the debate on the pros and cons of EMU is academic. The Finnish government could not influence the decision to initiate EMU according to schedule in 1999. That depended primarily on Germany and France. What remained for the Finnish government to decide was whether Finland should join EMU as a founding member or remain outside and wait and see how it turns out. The present Finnish government, under the leadership of Prime Minister Paavo Lipponen, the chairman of the Social Democratic Party, was determined to join in the first group.

The five-party "rainbow coalition" including the Social Democrats, the Conservative Party, the Left Alliance, the Greens, and the minority Swedish People's Party, set up after the April 1995 general election, made a sustained effort to ensure that Finland would meet the criteria for EMU membership in time for May 1998, when the heads of the EU governments made the final decision. Public spending has been cut by the equivalent of 10 percent of GDP since 1992. After the devaluation of the markka, an export-led boom has lifted the country out of the traumatic slump of 1991–1993. In the beginning of 1997, national output for the first time exceeded the levels it reached in the beginning of the decade. A revival of domestic demand and construction is now beginning. Growth reached 5.9 percent in 1997 and is expected to continue at a slightly lower level in 1998. Inflation is under 2 percent, and interest rates are close to German benchmark rates. The markka has been stable since 1995, enabling Finland to join the European exchange rate mechanism (ERM) in October 1996. Public debt is on its way down to the level of 60 percent of GDP, and the budget deficit is well within the 3 percent Maastricht limit.

According to a study published in March 1997 by the Swiss International Institute for Management Development (IMD), Finland has climbed to fourth place in comparative competitiveness, behind the United States, Singapore, and Hong Kong, and ahead of the Netherlands, Norway, and Denmark.[6] The IMD gives special credit to the high standard of science and technology and the educational level and the skills in the workforce in Finland. Although the forest industry still accounts for 25 percent of value-added in the manufacturing industry (and 11 percent of paper and board production in the entire EU area), the share of high-tech exports has risen to 16 percent of total exports, a level exceeded only by France among EU members. Finns are technology-minded, "the most wired country in the world," according to a *New York Times* report.[7] Nearly a third of Finland's 5 million people carry mobile phones, and the number increases by 27 percent a year.

According to a U.S. research service, Finland has 62 Internet-connected computers per thousand residents, a rate that is twice the U.S. rate. By the year 2000 all the country's 5,000 schools will be hooked to the Internet. Both government and private industry spending on research and development in the computer field is 2.9 percent of the GDP, and technology has a strong place in higher education.

The dark side of this success story is unemployment. The jobless rate is declining, but at a painfully slow pace. In spring 1998, it was 13.7 percent; if growth continues as expected, it may fall to 12 percent in 1999, which would still be above the EU average. One reason for this is the aftereffect of the collapse of the Soviet trade; generally, however, citizens of a small country who lose their jobs as a result of downsizing and mergers in industry and banking simply have fewer alternatives available to them: very few are able to take advantage of the freedom of movement within the EU.

Fundamentally, however, the job crisis in Finland is no different from the general crisis of the European welfare state. The Social Democratic system of welfare constructed during the decades of boom that followed World War II transformed capitalism from within, yet depended on capitalism to provide the jobs and the tax revenues: full employment was the cornerstone of the welfare state. Now capitalism, freed from the shackles of the nation-state, creates jobs wherever it is profitable. High-wage, high-tax European countries with tightly regulated labor markets are bound to lose out. The cry from the Left is "no surrender to market forces." Yet with interest on the public debt eating away 14 percent of tax revenues, as is the case in Finland, governments have no choice but to slim down the public sector. To fail to do so would raise interest rates, reduce investments, weaken competitiveness—leaving more people without jobs.

The transatlantic debate on jobs goes on in Finland too. Yes, we say, the United States produces more jobs, but it also produces a widening gap between the rich and the poor, more crime and drugs, and more dropouts from society. So the U.S. model is rejected as socially unacceptable. But then admittedly the European system is also leading to social injustice. The regulated labor markets divide workers into insiders and outsiders. The insiders have steady jobs and are protected by powerful trade unions and government regulations that limit layoffs. Outsiders depend on temporary or half-time jobs or unemployment benefits and ultimately welfare payments; an increasing number leave the labor force altogether, either because they despair of finding work or are induced to leave by early retirement or disability benefits.

President Jacques Chirac of France has suggested that a "third way" between the U.S. and European models must be found. Actually, Europe is already stumbling onto a third way. What this means is that labor market regulations that discourage companies from employing more people, as well as unemployment and other welfare benefits that tend to act as disincentives to job-seeking, are slowly being reduced through negotiations between governments, unions, and employers, while at the same time the existing system is being undermined or circumvented as more people are working in unprotected part-time or temporary jobs. Inevitably, income disparities and inequalities are growing. The welfare state is not being dismantled, but it is shrinking, partly by deliberate action from above, partly by erosion from below.

Quite apart from ideological inhibitions, political realities prevent any drastic change of policy in Finland. One such reality is the power of the labor unions. Finland's degree of unionization is still about 80 percent, second only to Sweden's. There is no conceivable political coalition in sight that would be prepared to face a head-on conflict with the unions. The political field is dominated by three parties that together command two-thirds of the total votes in parliamentary elections: the Social Democrats (28 percent in the 1995 elections), the Center Party (20 percent), and the Conservative Party (18 percent). The rest of the votes are divided between six groups—bit players on the parliamentary stage. Two of the three leading parties must be able to cooperate to form a majority coalition. After the 1987 elections, the government was formed by the Social Democrats and the Conservatives; in 1991, by the Center Party and the Conservatives; in 1995, by the Social Democrats and the Conservatives once again. It follows that neither a radical left-wing nor a Thatcherite right-wing policy is possible. The consensus built into the Finnish system makes politics a frustrating game. Yet political stability has been Finland's great strength in times of external danger and is a present strength as well, because it acts to counter social tension and potential conflict.

Joining EMU in the first group means a lifetime commitment to a German discipline in managing public finances: a frightening prospect to union leaders who believe that in a recession it would be less painful to lower real wages by devaluing the markka than by lowering nominal wages. But it is an illusion to believe that by staying outside Finland could have gained advantages at the expense of the insiders. It would be hit by currency speculation and high interest rates, while any attempt to play the old trick of devaluation would invite severe retaliation from the insiders.

Economic arguments aside, however, security in the broad sense of the term is once again the driving motive behind the Finnish government's decision to join EMU. By joining the inner sanctum of the European Union, Finland will make sure it will not be marginalized in a future crisis. In this view, the single currency will serve as a substitute for the security guarantees the Union has failed to provide: money as a bond thicker than blood.

In this respect, Finland's position differs fundamentally from that of Sweden and Denmark, neither of which looks upon the EU as a source of security. Denmark is a member of NATO; Sweden retains its faith in neutrality. The Finnish line has taken its partners by surprise. It had been widely expected that Finland would follow a "Nordic" course. British diplomats in particular have voiced disappointment that Finland has not clearly aligned itself with Britain on issues affecting the character of Union. In fact, Finns on the whole share the British view of the Union as an association of independent nation-states rather than as a community on its way to a federation. But the facts of geopolitics are what they are. When it comes to security, British interests do not extend to the Baltic region. Here Germany is dominant. Cynics might say that Finland can be relaxed about German-French proposals to "deepen" integration because it can depend on Britain to block them.

There is thus a contradiction in the Finnish attitude: Finland wants to be part of the core of the Union, but keeps open its options for the future. It seeks to maximize the advantages of membership with minimum sacrifice of sovereignty, but so does every member state. The contradiction is not confined to Finland: it is at the heart of the Union itself.

The debate on federalism tends to obscure rather than illuminate this underlying reality. The federalist idea was born in the aftermath of World War II in a divided Europe living under the threat of Soviet power—a time when the Western half of Germany could be described as a political dwarf while French leadership within the European Community went unchallenged. It was a time, too, when faith in the power of governments to shape the future was still strong. But this Europe no longer exists. United Germany is no longer a West European state: it is once again the central power on the European continent, with wide-ranging strategic and economic interests in Central and Eastern Europe and the Baltic region. The decision to move the capital to Berlin underlines the shift in German priorities. The German government worked hard to help Austria, Finland, and Sweden to join the European Union; Poland, the Czech Republic, Hungary, and Slovenia are next on the German list. The model is no longer Charlemagne's empire, but rather the Habsburg's—with Berlin instead of Vienna as center. The torch of federalism is now carried by Germany, which insists on "deepening" the Union as a necessary preamble to "widening" it.

I do not doubt the genuine commitment of the German elite to the European idea. They act in the spirit of Thomas Mann's famous slogan: Not a German Europe but a European Germany. Yet, as a citizen of a small state, I cannot help thinking that a German can afford the luxury of supporting an idealistic vision of a federal Europe, because he can be confident that his nation will always be strong enough to look after its own interests in whatever federal structure may be conceived. But a small nation like Finland cannot be sure that it would be able to maintain its vital national interests within a European federation. Significantly, Jean Monnet, the father of West European unity, favored decision making by a directorate of the major powers. He was "impatient of small countries," as a recent biographer has put it. "He used to quote with cheerful assent an anonymous prewar American who complained that in international conferences, whatever the agenda, the Norwegian delegate rose to talk of fish."[8] (Fish happened to be a vital interest for Norwegians in those days. Now it is oil and gas, no longer a laughing matter for the diplomats of the major powers.)

A telling argument against a European federation has been provided, inadvertently, by the French diplomat Jean-Marie Guehenno, whose book *La Fin de la Démocratie* was recently published in English under the title *The End of the Nation-State* without any change in the text. In Europe at any rate, the end of the nation-state would indeed mean the end of democracy as we know it. There is no substitute for the nation-state as a frame for a democratic society. The European idea is too distant and abstract to replace the nation as the focus of people's loyalty and solidarity. To drain the nation-state of its vitality would leave large parts of Europe's population rootless and disoriented. Europe's nation-states do need the Union to perform tasks none of them is able to cope with on its own. But the Union on its part needs as its members well-functioning nations-states capable of carrying out the policies jointly agreed upon.

The nation-state is not about to wither away. As long as the member states of the EU are able to collect roughly half of GDP in taxes, while passing on to the Union only 1.25 percent, they cannot be called powerless. The real problem in Europe is the inability of the Union to generate enough popular support for effective collective action. The remedy is not federalism, which is an intellectual or philosophical concept, not a political program. It is wise to "fear those big words which make us so unhappy." The future of Europe is not a choice between a federal state and a "glorified free trade area," which the British are supposed to favor. The Union as it is today has advanced far beyond a free trade area. The European Commission has certain supernational powers, and so has the European Court. The commission can take member governments to court if they disobey Union decisions, and the court's rulings are binding. The commission has a sole right of initiative in making proposals to the Council of Ministers, which represents the member governments, and it has sole competence in such areas as foreign trade policy and competition policy. It is about to acquire more powers to deal with international crime and problems of immigration. More decisions will be made by majority vote, and "flexibility" will enable groups of member states to deepen integration among themselves without waiting for everybody to go along. EMU will be a practical application of the principle of flexibility: not all the members will join from the beginning. Such reforms do not amount to federalism, but they will make it possible for member states to use the existing machinery more effectively.

Once the single currency has been adopted, closer coordination of economic policy will be necessary. On this point supporters of EMU tend to be vague or evasive so as not to frighten voters with the specter of a loss of sovereignty. Yet it stands to reason that monetary policy, to be determined by a "totally independent" European Central Bank, cannot be divorced from fiscal policies to be decided by each member government independently. In reality how independent will be the "totally independent" Central Bank? And how independently will member governments be able to conduct economic policy within EMU? No precise answers are possible before the new system has actually begun to function. In this sense EMU is a leap into the unknown—a crucial test for the future of the European Union itself.

# 5

# Security

A people's perceptions of national security are shaped less by rational calculation of future risks than by lessons drawn from past experiences. History influences Finnish opinion on national security in two seemingly contradictory ways. On the one hand, Finns wish to make sure their country will not be left alone once again to face a resurgence of Russian imperialism; on the other hand, they are skeptical about the willingness and ability of the West to come to their aid and want to avoid foreign entanglements that could draw the country into a conflict with Russia over issues unrelated to its vital interests. Finnish policy after the end of the Cold War has attempted to reconcile these two aspirations. By joining the European Union, Finland ensures that it will not be isolated in an international crisis; by refraining from seeking NATO membership, it has limited its risks and avoided upsetting Russia.

This policy makes Finland a unique case in Europe today. It is the only member of the European Union that has a common border with Russia, and the only European neighbor of the former Soviet Union that has not applied for NATO membership. The two distinctions are of course interrelated: because Finland is an EU member, it has not had an urgent need to join NATO.

EU membership, according to a Finnish government statement, "raises the threshold that would have to be surmounted in order to exert pressure on Finland." As Henry Kissinger has pointed out, "It is inconceivable that they [the EU member states] would ignore attacks on one of their members."[1] But because Finland thus relies on the bonds of solidarity that bind EU members to each other,

Finland itself could not remain neutral in a conflict between an EU member and a third party. Solidarity works both ways.

Yet EU solidarity is clearly limited, as revealed by Finland's relationship to the Western European Union (WEU), the defense alliance of the West European countries. Finland, like Austria and Sweden, has chosen observer status rather than membership in the WEU. The official explanation is that Finland prefers to stay outside of military alliances. The fact is, however, that it did not have any choice. The WEU is not prepared to admit new members unless they join NATO at the same time. What this means in plain language is that the major military powers in Western Europe—Britain, France, and Germany—will not commit themselves to the defense of Finland unless the United States, through NATO, underwrites their guarantee. So, while Finland relies on the EU, the EU relies on NATO.

Life in a borderland breeds ambiguity. Finland today is neither neutral nor allied. A further dimension is added to Finland's security policy by what has come to be called "the NATO option." As President Martti Ahtisaari told President Bill Clinton during the U.S.-Russian summit meeting in Helsinki in March 1997, the Finnish government does not exclude the possibility of applying for NATO membership in case circumstances change.

Finland is thus poised at the crossroads of two concepts of security that are partly overlapping and complementary, partly competing in post-Cold War Europe: the "soft" concept of security through integration within the EU and the "hard" security based on the military power of NATO under U.S. leadership.

## The Grand Design

The first flush of elation after the fall of the Berlin Wall seemed to bring universal agreement on the right road to peace and security. A grand design for a Europe united on the basis of common values was outlined in the Charter of Paris issued in November 1990 by the summit meeting of the Conference on Security and Cooperation in Europe. Peace and security, according to the Paris Charter, will be assured once all European nations have adopted the Western system of democracy and market economy. The common objective was to extend the security concept represented by the European Community to the Eastern half of Europe to promote political stability and economic prosperity and thereby create a reliable and lasting basis for the security of both halves. The Community had always claimed to be "Europe." During the Cold War it had had no choice but to remain an exclusively West European institution. Now at last it had the opportunity to make good its claim to represent all of Europe. No one spoke of any new role for NATO in this connection.

This vision of Europe's future reveals the enduring influence of eighteenth and nineteenth century German philosophy on political thought. To paraphrase John Maynard Keynes, politicians are often unaware that the opinion they express can be traced back to books written by professors they have never heard of. The notion that democracies do not make war against each other is derived from Immanuel Kant, who wrote 200 years ago that "eternal peace" would be attained when in every state decisions on war and peace were made by the citizens rather than by a single ruler. The claim that the Western system of government has universal validity echoes Hegel's thesis of the "end of history." And present-day faith in the capacity of the market to transform the former socialist societies recalls Karl Marx's prediction that the capitalist system would force all nations to use the same method of production and thus "create a world of its own image."

Had the political leaders gathered in Paris consulted historians rather than philosophers they might have shown greater caution. The nations emerging from the ruins of Soviet power have little in common except the fate they shared as victims of the conflict between German and Russian imperialism, followed by forced integration into the Soviet system. During this century, every country of what is called Central and Eastern Europe has been devastated by war, occupied, liberated, and reoccupied, each time with a change of political system and in many cases also of borders. After the breakup of the Soviet Union and Yugoslavia, the number of sovereign state members of the United Nations that now fill the space between Trieste and the Urals has risen to 23. Only six of these were in existence before 1918: Russia, Romania, Bulgaria, Albania, Greece, and Turkey. Several came into existence after World War I; others since 1989, including several countries that had never in history had the status of independent statehood in the modern sense, or that had it briefly—for a year or two, for a decade or two—and then lost it, although some have since regained it: the three Baltic states, Belarus, Ukraine, Slovakia, Moldova, Slovenia,

Croatia, Macedonia. Parliamentary democracy and the market economy have never had a strong constituency in these countries. Before World War II, Czechoslovakia and Austria were the only democracies and industrial states among them. All the others were predominantly agrarian countries ruled by authoritarian regimes. Once Soviet power was withdrawn and the uniformity imposed by Moscow broke down, the ancient differences, rivalries, and feuds reemerged. The mentality of the people shaped by the past cannot easily be reformed, as has been found in Eastern Germany, the former German Democratic Republic, which in spite of generous subsidies from West Germany still lags behind.

As the full extent of the devastation, physical and moral, caused by Soviet rule has unfolded, the vision of a united Europe seemed far removed from the brutal realities prevailing in the eastern half of the continent. At the time the Charter of Paris was issued, it was possible to believe that a dynamic, self-confident Western community would exercise, in countless different ways, a powerful influence on developments throughout the former Soviet empire. But today Western Europe itself is in crisis. Victory in the ideological contest of the Cold War has paradoxically made Western nations more critical of their own system. Now that the rival system has collapsed, they can no longer console themselves with Winston Churchill's famous dictum—that democracy is a poor way to govern a country, but less so than any known alternative. Wracked by self-doubt and pessimism, the European Union has been slow to tackle the task of extending its reach eastward.

Before widening can be carried out, the EU has to be "deepened": decision-making procedures must be adjusted to accommodate a larger number of participants. In June 1997, some modest progress was achieved, allowing for 5 of the 12 countries that have applied for membership to begin accession negotiations. (In addition, talks with Cyprus will also begin, but this is a special case, the solution of which will depend on agreement between Turkey and Greece on the future of the island state.) The five countries selected by the European Commission for the first round are the Czech Republic, Estonia, Hungary, Poland, and Slovenia. But the gap between the 5 and the present 15 members of the EU remains wide. The most prosperous of the applicants is Slovenia, with its per capita income of 59 percent of the EU average; the poorest Estonia, with 22 percent. How much money the EU will have available to help the applicants will not be known until the

Union's budget criteria have been revised in 1999. The accession process will obviously take many years. In the meantime the rest of the applicants (Bulgaria, Latvia, Lithuania, Romania, and Slovakia) will receive further tuition from the European Commission to prepare them for membership. But how far east can the EU stretch itself? General de Gaulle spoke of Europe from "the Atlantic to the Urals"—a phrase of calculated ambiguity. Today, too, political leaders speak in ambiguous terms, although less by calculation than through indecision. The eastern border of Europe as a community of shared values—Immanuel Kant's Europe—remains clouded in uncertainty.

## The Balkan War

In the meantime, the vision of the Paris Charter was shattered by the breakup of the Federation of Yugoslavia and the savage war between its peoples. As a result, Europe's post-Cold War "security architecture" had to be redesigned.

At first, the Western governments were inclined to look at the fighting in the former Yugoslavia as one more chapter in the long history of merciless strife between the Balkan peoples—an internal war not amenable to outside influences. The historical roots of the conflict are indeed striking, as was revealed by the republication of the report of an international inquiry into the Balkan war of 1912–1913 commissioned by the Carnegie Endowment for International Peace. The deliberate use of military action for the extermination of civilian populations, the destruction of towns and villages, the atrocities committed by all sides against women and children, the total lack of willingness to compromise: in all these respects the Balkan war of 1993–1997 was a repetition of 1912–1913.

In his introduction to the new edition of the Carnegie report, George Kennan concludes that

> what we are up against is the sad fact that the developments of those earlier ages . . . had the effect of thrusting into the south-eastern reaches of the European continent a salient of non-European civilization that has continued to the present day to preserve many of its non-European characteristics, including some that fit even less with the world of today than they did with the world of eighty years ago.[2]

   This is an unfashionable opinion in our age of integration, which tends to gloss over ethnic or cultural differences between peoples, but as such a useful antidote to the tendency of political analysts and commentators to leap from a particular event to a general theory. The Balkan peoples are, of course, not the only Europeans capable of aggressive behavior. As Kennan points out, we are dealing with relative distinctions. But there is nowhere in Europe a concatenation of historical, ethnic, and religious conflicts comparable to the viper's nest in the Balkans.

   It seemed little had changed in Europe since the days of Otto von Bismarck, chancellor of the newly united Germany, who in December 1876 made his famous remark that Germany had no interest in the Eastern Question, as the Balkan conflict of that time was called, "that was worth the healthy bones of a single Pomeranian grenadier."[3] President Bill Clinton, in an unguarded moment, put it less eloquently: "Until these folks get tired of killing each other over there, bad things will continue to happen."[4]

   Yet the Western governments, harassed by the media, did not succeed in keeping aloof. Recognition of the independence of Slovenia and Croatia was the first step on the slippery slope. We shall never know what might have been achieved had the major powers made recognition conditional upon a prior peaceful settlement, under international auspices, of borders, minority rights, and other contested issues. What we do know is that the reflexive application of the principle of national self-determination virtually forced the Muslim population of Bosnia-Herzegovina, a religious rather than a national or ethnic community that had never aspired to become a nation-state, to seek independence to avoid being left at the mercy of Serbian ambitions. The struggle between the peoples of the former Federation of Yugoslavia was thus transformed into a war between sovereign states: the UN could not stand aside.

   What followed is a familiar story. The UN intervention progressed from mediation to arms embargo, economic sanctions, humanitarian missions to protect the civilian population, finally selected air strikes by NATO planes—anything short of the kind of action that might risk substantial casualties.

   What distinguished the current Balkan crisis from earlier ones is the role of the media. Yet the pressure of public opinion has been ambiguous. People were revolted by television reports of atrocities and demanded that something be done to stop them. But in no European country were people urging their government to send their own soldiers to do the job. They said: Let the UN or NATO do something. This is a way of asking someone else to do what one is not prepared to do oneself. The initials of international organizations remain abstractions unless brought to life by the national will of the member states. This will has been lacking.

Bismarck, once again, said it: "I have always found the word Europe on the lips of those politicians who wanted something from other powers which they dare not demand in their own names."[5]

On an intellectual level, the critics of Western policy made a persuasive case by arguing that not only humanitarian concerns but fundamental European interests are at stake in the Balkans, and that the failure to act forcefully has undermined Europe's credibility throughout Central and Eastern Europe, including Russia. But such a calculation of the long-term interests of Europe failed to touch the emotional chords of people living in conditions of security and relative affluence.

European societies today simply have no stomach for the kind of large-scale military interventions that would have had to be mounted in the former Yugoslavia. Whether this is due to a general weakening of loyalty to the state, hedonistic individualism, or simply the small size of families, as Edward Luttwak has claimed, remains for sociologists to analyze.[6] The political consequences are already evident. Politicians are haunted by the specter of body bags flown back from distant battlefields to grieving relatives. In a memorable scene on British television, the weeping mother of a soldier killed in Bosnia said to reporters: "And I was so happy when he joined the army—we thought it was a secure job." The spirit is no longer what it used to be in the days of Tennyson: "Theirs not to reason why/Theirs but to do and die" (*The Charge of the Light Brigade*).

At the beginning of the fighting, the president of the European Union had proclaimed the opportunity to stop the wars of Yugoslav dissolution "the hour of Europe." The United States stood aside; it was a European problem. But Washington did not remain a detached bystander. Although refusing to get directly involved, the United States undermined the compromises offered by European mediators. But when it was finally realized that the use of force was necessary to make diplomacy work, the United States played the decisive role in stopping the fighting and bullying the warring parties into accepting the Dayton Accords on November 21, 1995. And the U.S. military contribution was, and still is, decisive in policing the implementation of the Dayton Accords and in the international effort to help to build peace in the shattered land.

The message of the Yugoslav tragedy for the nations of Central and Eastern Europe was grim. "The hour of Europe" had revealed the limits of the will and ability of the West European countries to use force in defense of common values and collective security outside the area they are committed by treaty to defend. The power of the United States was still needed in Europe. That is why Russia's neighbors are now striving to be admitted to NATO. They desperately wish to be accepted, to belong. They cannot dismiss the possibility, as President Vaclav Havel of the Czech Republic has put it, "that in Russia forces still enamored of the imperial ambitions of the former Soviet Union would temporarily gain the upper hand: chauvinist, Great Russian, cryptocommunist and cryptototalitarian forces." Because admission into the European Union obviously will take many years, joining NATO offers a shortcut into the Western fold.

Western critics of NATO enlargement argue that fears of a resurgence of Russian aggressiveness are exaggerated. That Russia is weak today is obvious, and it is a fallacy to imagine that Russia could become strong again by reverting to a closed command economy and a militarized foreign policy—in other words, by methods that led to the downfall of the Soviet Union. The imperialist rhetoric emanating from Moscow only shows that Russian politicians have learned to shout when arguing a weak point. For a long time to come, Russia will lack the strength to play an important role in world affairs.

The poor showing of the Russian army in the war in Chechnya is often cited as proof of Russia's inability to resume its imperial role. But the war in Chechnya also revealed that Russia still has the will to use force to squash the independence of a small people; the brutal behavior familiar from earlier times has not changed. For someone like myself who has been on the receiving end of a Russian assault, the reports from Chechnya sounded depressingly familiar. This could be overlooked by those living at a safe distance. Indeed, the Russian onslaught on Chechnya has been excused by Western governments as an internal matter, a permissible act to put down a secessionist rebellion, or even as a law enforcement operation against smugglers and black marketeers. But for people living in the neighborhood, Chechnya serves as a sinister warning. For as a regional power Russia retains a massive preponderance over its European neighbors, and Russia's weakness in the global context has the paradoxical effect of sharpening the security concerns of these countries, because it tends to lessen Western interest in this region. They have not forgotten all that Yalta stands for.

What actually took place at the Yalta conference is beside the point. The name of the place is engraved upon the collective memory of the people in Central and Eastern Europe as the symbol of the West's willingness at the end of World War II to accept Soviet domination in that part of Europe, believing, as President Franklin Roosevelt once wrote, that Stalin's early education for the priesthood had "entered into his nature something of the way in which a Christian gentleman should behave."[7]

During his visit to Prague in January 1994, President Bill Clinton was asked by a Czech reporter whether it was conceivable, given the lessons of history, that NATO would fail to come to the aid of an East European country if it were invaded or subject to military aggression. Clinton replied, according to agency reports, that he thought it was "doubtful" that there would be no help. "I think your reading of our history is right," he said.[8]

One wonders what history he had in mind. The history the people in Prague remember is one of Western indifference to their fate. At the end of World War II, the West acquiesced to Soviet hegemony over Central and Eastern Europe. The Cold War was not caused by what happened east of the line that cut across Germany, but by the fear that Soviet military power combined with Communist subversion posed a direct threat to Western societies themselves until 1963. Former president Valéry Giscard d'Estaing of France has recently written, "We were still living with the fear of a Soviet invasion, and the whole political vocabulary suggested we could wake up one morning occupied by herds of Soviets."[9] The Soviet domain was never seriously challenged by the West. Even in the dying days of the Soviet empire, President George Bush and other Western leaders preferred stability, which meant helping Mikhail Gorbachev to stay in power: they did not encourage East Europeans to seek their freedom. Now that the ideological contest is over and Russia is weak, the West might turn its back on what happens in those "far-away countries." The Poles and the others want to join NATO, not only because they fear a possible resurgence of Russian power, but because they do not trust the West without ironclad written guarantees.

Initially, the desire of the former members of the Warsaw Pact to join NATO was received with embarrassment, both in the United States and in Western Europe. The general view was that NATO had done its job of maintaining the balance of power and thus deterring a Soviet aggression. NATO now could retire into the background as a last reserve against the unlikely eventuality of a renewal of the Russian threat. An enlargement of the military alliance, in this view, would be irrelevant to the real problems of the countries clamoring for membership. They did not face a military threat, but rather the danger of being sucked into the vortex of economic backwardness and social instability caused by the legacy of 50 years of Soviet rule. Against this, NATO was no defense. Surely an extension of the European Union was the right answer. There was also the problem of reconciling two incompatible policies: to treat Russia as a peaceful partner and to protect Poland and other countries against possible Russian aggression.

The first attempt to solve the dilemma was the scheme called the Partnership for Peace (PfP), enabling NATO to initiate military cooperation with nonmember countries, ostensibly to develop joint crisis management and peacekeeping capabilities. Its reception varied in accordance with the level of expectations in each of the countries concerned. Those who feared they might be left on the wrong side of the new line welcomed PfP as better than nothing—a cup half full. But those who hoped to be admitted to membership were disappointed—a cup half empty. The Poles in particular felt let down, like a suitor who is proposing marriage and is offered platonic friendship instead. The reason why they wished to join NATO was not an ardent interest in peacekeeping; it was the desire to receive the security guarantee contained in Article 5 of the North Atlantic Treaty.

## The New Enemy

Suddenly, in the midst of all the doubts and hesitations, President Clinton charged ahead: It was not a question of whether NATO would admit new members, he declared, only when and how. He said this in Prague on January 12, 1994. Was it a spontaneous response to what his audience so fervently longed to hear? Whatever his motives, this was the decisive step. To retreat would have been one more betrayal of the nations struggling to find a secure place in the space vacated by Soviet power.

Clinton's when and how turned out to mean "an extensive study" on all aspects of a possible enlargement. But as usual, unforeseen events forced the politicians' hand. NATO's operation in Bosnia became a catalyst of change that reverberated throughout Europe.

Until then, doubts about NATO's relevance to the post-Cold War security needs of Europe had persisted. When Soviet leader Mikhail Gorbachev had begun to apply his "new thinking" to foreign policy in the late 1980s, Georgi Arbatov, the Kremlin's spin doctor, issued his memorable threat to NATO: "We will do something terrible to you—we will deprive you of your enemy." The loss of an enemy has usually been fatal to a military alliance; it either falls apart or just withers away. But the Bosnian tragedy helped NATO to discover a new enemy. Not one identified by his flag or the shape of his helmets, yet recognized by every government in Europe: the new enemy is instability. Like a modern version of the Holy Alliance, NATO now aspires to become the guardian of order in a Europe united by common values, with democracy and the market economy recognized as the only legitimate system for European states. Thus treating Russia as a partner and admitting new members to NATO could be reconciled; surely Russia, too, would benefit from order and stability along its western borders.

The U.S. move had a bandwagon effect nobody had been able to foresee. Once U.S. troops began moving into Bosnia, every other country in Europe, and some outside, wanted to join. For the first time in history, troops from neutral and nonaligned countries were prepared to serve under NATO command. Even Russia could not stand aside.

NATO's new mission has been described by U.S. officials in truly missionary terms. According to national security adviser Sandy Berger, "the goal is to assert that America is a European power, with plans to build an undivided, peaceful, democratic Europe." And in the words of former U.S. ambassador to NATO Robert Hunter:

> What the European Union and NATO are trying to do in Central Europe is nothing less than to complete the promise of the Marshall Plan, which was thwarted by Joseph Stalin some fifty years ago and bounded at the iron curtain. We now have a chance finally take that grand effort to completion. How rare it is in history—perhaps unique—that we have a chance to take a second bite at history's apple. . . . [10]

From a European point of view, former secretary of state Warren Christopher used a key phrase in his farewell address on January 15, 1997, when he spoke of the United States as "the indispensable nation" in the twenty-first century.[11] It was indispensable because the European nations have not found the common will to use their great resources for their own defense, lagging far behind the United States in military technology. Like a patient who dares not walk without crutches even after being healed, the European Union still depends on the United States for security, relieved now by the reaffirmation of the U.S. commitment to Europe, yet as always resentful toward its protector.

A further sign of the change in Europe was the decision of the neo-Gaullist president of France Jacques Chirac to declare conscription obsolete: a dramatic break with tradition in a country that had been the first to introduce conscription 200 years ago. This revealed the geopolitical divide that cuts across Europe. The nations living behind the back of united Germany no longer need to be prepared to defend their borders against an invading army. The fear that they "could wake up one morning occupied by herds of Soviets" has faded away. For them, security now requires the capacity to project force to crisis points outside their own country, and for this they need professional soldiers, not conscripts. But the nations living between Germany and Russia—Finland, for instance—cannot yet afford to scrap the revolutionary French concept of *lever en masse*. What Napoleon said 200 years ago is still true: geography determines a country's foreign policy.

President Chirac then went on to disown Charles de Gaulle by rejoining NATO's political organs: a step based on a realistic analysis of the state of the European Union. As Foreign Minister Hervé de Charette pointed out, "Europe is far from having demonstrated its strength on the defense front." Its own defense alliance, the Western European Union, "has responsibilities but no capabilities." The logical conclusion was to work within NATO to ensure that the formidable assets of the alliance could be used for safeguarding European interests, even in situations in which the United States might not be willing to get directly involved. At the time of writing, no agreement has been reached on the modalities of a French return to the military system of NATO, but this is less important than the fact that France now takes part in the political cooperation within the alliance.[12]

Although the French are more interested in reforming NATO,

or "Europeanizing" it, than in enlarging it, Germany is America's principal partner in the effort to bring the three Central European countries—the Czech Republic, Hungary, and Poland—into the alliance. After half a century of frontline duty, the Germans understandably wish to be relieved. In the bad old days it would have been said that Germany wishes to create a belt of buffer states between Russia and itself. Today it is politically correct to describe the enlargement as an eastern complement to Germany's western integration.

German investments in Poland, Hungary, and the Czech Republic have grown so dramatically since 1990 that the three countries are now collectively known as "Germany's backyard." In addition to private investments, they have collected more than $100 billion in aid from Bonn since the iron curtain fell in 1989 and have shifted the entire focus of their economies toward the West. German capital now employs several million workers in this backyard. The invasion of private German firms is creating jobs and prosperity, allaying old fears of German domination. Grossdeutschland—greater Germany—is thus emerging in the shape of a benevolent giant. Itself a semipacifist society where more than half the young men liable to military training refuse to bear arms and choose civilian service instead, Germany is intent on spreading the gospel of political stability and economic progress to the East, making every effort to reassure Russia on the peaceful character of New NATO.

The Russian political establishment does not easily let itself be reassured. Because Russians have always been swayed by political paranoia and conspiracy theories, it is likely that some of them really believe what they say about the threat posed by NATO enlargement. The Russian attitude has often been explained in psychological terms as expressions of wounded pride, to be treated with diplomatic psychotherapy, like gestures designed to prove that the West still looks upon Russia as a superpower. Wounded pride probably does play a part, but there is a more down-to-earth explanation. NATO enlargement will irrevocably shrink the scope of Moscow's influence in what used to be its "outer empire," confirming the reduced status of Russia. Poland, the pivotal country, will finally be out of Moscow's reach: a historical shift in Europe's geopolitical structure. However much the leaders of NATO talk about their desire of partnership with Russia in the defense of democracy, the fact remains that NATO enlargement settles the score of the Cold War. This is how the majority of the Russian establishment sees it.

The Russian opposition to NATO enlargement has united the entire political spectrum, from extreme nationalists to reformist liberals, which shows that Russia has not changed that much. Not for the first time, Russian diplomacy has managed to turn weakness into an asset. By warning the West that enlargement would bring out the worst in Russia, Moscow has employed a traditional tactic. Even Stalin used to warn the West that if his proposals were rejected, dark forces lurking somewhere in the background would take over and make the West's life even worse. As things have turned out, Russia has in fact succeeded in extracting maximum concessions for something they could not have prevented anyway.

## New NATO and New Russia

The bargain struck at the summit meeting of presidents Bill Clinton and Boris Yeltsin on March 21, 1997, in Helsinki, was hailed as a historic settlement. Russia was assured that no nuclear weapons or allied troops will be deployed in the territories of NATO's new member states, and the joint NATO-Russia Council was set up to provide for consultation and coordination and, whenever possible, joint decision making in action on security issues. But the statements by the two presidents revealed fundamental differences in their approach.

According to Clinton, the principal challenge faced by the summit meeting was "building an undivided, democratic and peaceful Europe for the first time in history." He went on to state that NATO—"New NATO"—was the bedrock of Europe's security and that Russia would become its respected partner "in making the future for all Europe peaceful and secure." But Yeltsin said nothing about an undivided democratic Europe. For him, the summit demonstrated that "our countries [the United States and Russia] occupy such a position in the world that global issues are the subject of our discussions." He was referring to the arms control agreements on the summit agenda. The Helsinki meeting, according to Yeltsin, "opened a new stage in Russian-American relations." He thus spoke in the spirit of a new superpower condominium over Europe. Significantly, neither president mentioned the European Union. Europe was absent when the future European security order was discussed, and in essence settled, by the leaders of the United States and Russia.

How the NATO-Russia Joint Council will be able to reconcile the differences in approach remains to be seen. According to Clinton, Russia will have a voice but not a veto; according to Yeltsin, decisions will be made by consensus. While in the West security has been sublimated into crisis management and peacemaking or peacekeeping, Russians still speak about it in the traditional terms of hard defense, military blocs, and spheres of influence.

The U.S.-Russian summit in Helsinki was followed by the NATO-Russian summit in June in Paris and by the grand finale in July in Madrid where the decision was made to begin membership negotiations with the Czech Republic, Hungary, and Poland. The Euro-Atlantic Partnership Council (EAPC) was established comprising all the 43 states with which NATO has Partnership for Peace agreements.

Thus, a new European "security architecture" has finally taken shape, although not as a result of the deliberate implementation of a coherent strategy, but rather through a series of improvised responses to unforeseen events. No wonder it has turned into something quite different from what anyone had originally imagined. It is a U.S.-designed, open-ended, split-level structure, with the upper floor reserved for consultations between New NATO and New Russia, while down below Old NATO will watch out in case Old Russia rears its head. Upstairs, the spirit of Woodrow Wilson reigns. But this time the United States is hedging its bet on a triumph of democracy by keeping the military alliance intact as guarantor of the balance of power. A marriage of the two concepts of security—the soft and the hard—has been consummated.

The new European order is of course still subject to ratification by the U.S. Senate. The stage is set for one of those great debates by which Americans from time to time redefine their relationship to Europe. And once again Europeans find themselves in the humiliating position of having no vote and not much of a voice in decisions of vital importance to their security.

What can a European say to Americans who wonder why still today, almost a decade after the collapse of the Soviet Union, Americans should risk war to protect people living in Central and East European cities with unpronounceable names? He can only mumble something about shared values and common history.

European opinion has failed to grasp that the U.S. debate on

NATO enlargement is not a traditional contest between isolationists and internationalists. Opponents to enlargement can be found in both camps, and the issues are more ambiguous than in Cold War debates.

Russia today is no longer an adversary to be contained or pressed back, but is considered a partner to be trusted and supported. Even more important, Russia is America's neighbor—in space. Russia is still the only country with the capacity to inflict terrible damage on the U.S. continent and its people. Understandably, Clinton considered the arms control agreements reached at the Helsinki summit as his greatest achievement. "Now think about it," he exclaimed at the postsummit press conference. "Within a decade we will have reduced both sides' strategic nuclear arsenals by 80 percent below their Cold War peak of just five years ago." But now critics of his policy claim that NATO enlargement endangers his achievement by turning political opinion in Russia against the United States, putting ratification of arms control agreements by the Russian Duma at risk. Russian hard-liners would probably have opposed these agreements in any case; as the former Russian foreign minister Andrei Kozyrev has pointed out, they need an external enemy to justify their opposition to democratic reforms. But of course NATO enlargement has played into their hands.[13]

This part of the U.S. debate has received little attention in Europe. On another level, however, U.S. opponents to enlargement have their counterparts in Europe. On both sides of the Atlantic, an influential part of political opinion opposes by reflex action any scheme that enhances the role of the military. NATO is the wrong solution to the problems of Central and Eastern Europe, it is said. The former Soviet satellites are not threatened by military aggression; instead of making them spend more money on their armed forces, these countries should receive assistance for economic and social reform. In this way, the argument goes, Russian reformers, too, would be encouraged.

The historical dimension of this line of reasoning has been brought to light by the intervention of George Kennan, who has called NATO enlargement a great mistake. The father of the concept of containment, Kennan was a sharp critic of what he considered the excessive militarization of the U.S. effort to contain Soviet power. Now, at the age of 93, Kennan once again warns against a militarization of U.S. policy toward Russia.

Many Europeans no doubt agree with him, but at the same

time want the United States to stay in Europe. They cannot have it both ways. NATO's new mission ensures continued U.S. engagement in the task of building security in post-Cold War Europe. It also helps to maintain the balance between the growing power of united Germany and its European allies, but this may be too subtle an argument to have much influence in public debate.

In politics as in law, nine-tenths of the solution is provided by the facts on the ground. The most powerful argument in favor of NATO enlargement is that the process of admitting three new members—the Czech Republic, Hungary, and Poland—has been carried so far that it simply cannot be reversed. A refusal by the U.S. Senate to ratify the accession of these three states would not restore the situation that existed before they were invited to join, but would seriously undermine the credibility of U.S. policy in Europe, send shock waves throughout Central and Eastern Europe, and encourage Russian hard-liners to believe Moscow could regain its old sphere of influence. It seems safe to bet that the first round of enlargement will be ratified.

But this would not be the end of matter. The real battle will be fought on what comes next: Will more nations enter NATO within a reasonable period of time? Will the next round be put off indefinitely or for such a long time that the political effect would be tantamount to closing the door?

## The Open Door

The stand of the U.S. administration is unequivocal. President Clinton has repeatedly stated that NATO's door must remain open. Secretary of State Madeleine Albright has said that every democratic country will be eligible "whatever its location on the map of Europe." This position is in keeping with the idealistic tradition of a missionary foreign policy committed to spreading American values across the world. The door must remain open because were it to be closed, the effect would be to divide Europe into spheres of influence—an outcome abhorrent to the Wilsonians and, because it would be regarded as a victory for Russia, unacceptable to adherents of the realist school of foreign policy as well.

This built-in dynamic in NATO's enlargement policy remains a potential cause of friction in relations with Russia. Moscow has already drawn a line in the sand: Russia will in no circumstances accept the inclusion of former Soviet republics in NATO. This is a new version of the Brezhnev doctrine, although Foreign Minister Yevgeniy Primakov has explained that it would not be enforced the way it was in 1968, when Czechoslovakia was occupied.

The most important former Soviet republic is of course Ukraine, a nation of 52 million in the heart of Europe and a neighbor of Poland, which will soon be a NATO member. The West, particularly the United States and Germany, has invested heavily in Ukraine, both economically and politically. NATO has given Ukraine a special status among its "partners for peace," and Ukraine is now the third largest beneficiary of U.S. aid, after Israel and Egypt. Yet its standard of living has plummeted, while senior officials have become multimillionaires. Corruption is said to be remarkable even by the standards of the region. But the problems of the country go deeper. In addition to having a Russian minority of 10 million, the Ukrainian people themselves are divided by religion and language, torn between the appeal of the glittering lights of Europe and the undertow of Slavic unity. Ukraine's relations with Russia are further complicated by the dispute over Crimea. The notion that Ukraine, the cradle of the Orthodox faith, might defect to the Western camp is dismissed by Russians as unthinkable, and to the relief of both Moscow and NATO, the Ukrainian leadership has refrained from applying for membership either in NATO or the EU.

But the three Baltic states—Estonia, Latvia, and Lithuania—are seeking membership in both NATO and the EU, and this will present a serious challenge to NATO-Russian relations in the coming years. For Finland, and for Sweden as well, it is a vital interest to support the claim of the three Baltic states for a place in the Western structures. As long as they remain outside, the Baltic region as a whole remains unsettled, and the role of Finland and Sweden themselves in the European security order will be subject to speculation.

Some U.S. officials dealing with the Baltic issue seem to believe that in time "the wolf will lie down with the lamb"—that Russia will overcome its suspicions of the New NATO and will no longer oppose its extension to the Baltic states. As deputy secretary of state Strobe Talbott has put it, the Russians should be persuaded to look to the thirteenth-century Hansa League as a model for the Baltic region's future, one in which the Baltic states would not be an invasion route inward, but a gateway outward.[14] At present, however, there are little grounds for such optimism. True, in the Russian view the Baltic countries are not comparable to Ukraine. What ties them to Russia is not blood and faith; it is history and the imperial mentality that lives on in Russia. According to opinion surveys, Peter the Great, the conqueror of the Baltic coast, is still regarded by Russians as the most popular leader of all times. Even Mikhail Gorbachev shared the belief in the unique organic character of the Russian empire within which the smaller nations, like the Baltics, were protected, not oppressed, by their big brother, the Russian people.[15]

The present leadership in Moscow appears reconciled to the independence of the three Baltic states, and there is no reason to suspect that it might use force against them. But it objects to letting the Baltic states join NATO on the ground that it would be contrary to Russia's "legitimate security interests." The real reason may well be psychological rather than military. NATO's presence in the Baltic countries would effectively destroy the credibility of Russia's aspiration to regain the status of a great power—the ultimate humiliation.

In the U.S.-Baltic "Charter of Cooperation" confirmed in Washington on January 16, 1998, the United States committed itself to supporting the admission of the three Baltic states into NATO. Given the Russian attitude, however, this promise seems hollow. In theory, Russia will not have a veto, but in practice Russia's voice within the NATO-Russia Council may well be strong enough to dissuade NATO from going further, especially as there will not be much pressure within NATO itself for taking in additional members. German interests will be satisfied by the inclusion of Poland and the former Habsburg lands. Other NATO states have even less interest in an eastward expansion.

An argument often heard is that admitting the Baltic states would be a provocative challenge to Russia's security interests, implying that Moscow has real grounds to fear an invasion by NATO forces. Another argument is that the Baltic states are "indefensible." But during the Cold War, West Berlin was surely indefensible and so was Denmark, but Moscow knew that an attack against either would unleash a third world war. Those who say that the Baltic states are indefensible actually mean that in their case NATO is not prepared to risk war.

At this point the two concepts of security exchange roles: NATO pauses and the EU steps forward. The idea is that EU membership would reassure the Baltic nations and stabilize the region without provoking Russia. So far at any rate, the Russian government has not voiced any opposition to enlarging the EU up to its border, which happened when Finland joined.

But getting the Baltic states into the EU is easier said than done. The three countries are not identical triplets. The Latvian and Lithuanian languages are related, while Estonian is a Finno-Ugric language close to Finnish. In religion, Estonia and Latvia are predominantly Lutheran; Lithuania is Roman Catholic. For histori-cal reasons, Estonia and Latvia regard themselves as part of the Nordic cultural sphere, while Lithuania's history is closely linked to Poland's, and a sizable Polish minority still lives in Lithuania. There are also differences in the strategic situations of the three countries. Lithuania permits the transit of Russian armed forces to and from the Russian base in Kaliningrad, while in Latvia Russia still maintains a radar facility. Only Estonia is now completely free of Russian military influence.

Because the per capita income of the three Baltic states is still low—in Estonia 22 percent of the EU average, in Latvia 18 percent, and in Lithuania 24 percent—it is not possible for all three to be included among the five candidates for admission in the first round. For this reason, the Finnish government has vigorously campaigned for at least one Baltic state to be included among the first, on the ground that in this way the EU would demonstrate that the Baltic nations will not be left in a no-man's-land between Europe and Russia. The obvious choice as the spearhead is Estonia, a country closely related to Finland by history, language, and culture, and now becoming rapidly integrated into the Finnish economy.

The European Union has reached the same conclusion. Its agenda for EU enlargement designates Estonia as one of the five countries in the first round of enlargement. Although its GDP figure is still low, Estonia has made progress in other areas. According to the report of the European Commission, Estonia is a democratic state with institutions that safeguard the rule of law and respect for human rights. It is also a functioning market economy.

The commission effectively refutes Russian allegations that the Russian minority in Estonia is badly treated. Almost 35 percent of the population are non-Estonian, most of them Russians. They have representatives in Parliament, and even those who are not yet Estonian citizens can vote in local elections. They may use their own language in court and in dealing with authorities in areas where they are in the majority. They also have their own newspapers and radio and television programs. Altogether, according to the commission, minority rights are respected, and relations between Russians and Estonians are peaceful.

The main problem is that relatively few Russians have acquired Estonian citizenship. According to Estonian law, a condition of naturalization is adequate knowledge of the Estonian language and of the country's history and constitution; this requirement seems to be an obstacle to some of the Russians residing in Estonia. Psychological factors are perhaps more important than legal provisions, on both sides. Only seven years ago the Russians living in the Baltic states were part of the ruling people of the Soviet Union and felt no need to learn the language of the country, while the Estonians were victims of 50 years of oppression designed to eradicate their cultural and linguistic identity. Understandably, Estonians now insist on a language test as a form of commitment on the part of Russians applying for citizenship. Opinion surveys show that among the younger generations of Russians many are prepared to integrate themselves into Estonian society. But the older people live suspended between the past and the present, not wishing to leave Estonia where they are better off than they would be in Russia, yet unwilling to reconcile themselves to their changed status and encouraged by the harsh rhetoric emanating from Moscow to hope that the good old days might come back again.

The European Commission urges the Estonian government to provide more language courses for Russians and take other measures to speed up naturalization procedures. The prospect of joining the EU has already acted as a spur to reforms in this and other areas. The accession negotiations will no doubt take a long time, perhaps six or seven years or even longer, but the process itself enhances Estonia's status in two important respects: it makes the country a more reliable prospect for investors and business partners and ensures that any Russian attempt to pressure Estonia will instantly become an international issue.

## Finland and Sweden: In or Out?

For Finland, Estonia's progress toward EU membership is an obvious gain in security. It also brings additional responsibility. Finland will assume its share of the EU solidarity that will be extended to Estonia. Almost unnoticed, Finnish foreign policy has evolved a long way from the neutrality of the Cold War days. In 1990, for instance, when Estonians were struggling to gain their freedom, President Koivisto made it quite clear that they could not expect any assistance from Finland. Today, Finnish serving officers are advising the Estonian defense forces, and Estonian officers are being trained in Finland.

Is this as far as Finland will go, or will it call its "NATO option" in the near future? I can claim to have been the first to initiate a serious debate on this question.

In a speech in May 1996 at a meeting of a society devoted to national security, I suggested that NATO enlargement and the establishment of NATO-Russia security cooperation would induce first Austria and then Sweden and Finland to join NATO, not from fear of a Russian military aggression, but because staying outside would marginalize their influence in decisions affecting their own security. Austria, Finland, and Sweden, I said, would face a choice similar to the one posed in 1989 when Jacques Delors offered economic cooperation without membership in the European Union. The Partnership for Peace program was a comparable offer: military cooperation with NATO without security guarantees. The three countries would be without a seat at the table where the decisions on European security would be made—to paraphrase the argument used by President Koivisto in support of Finland's decision to apply for EU membership.

The debate triggered by my speech continues in all three countries. Understandably it is most intense in Austria. Once the first stage of NATO enlargement has been carried out, Austria will be physically within NATO territory. The "permanent neutrality" inscribed into its constitution will become an empty phrase. A cynic might say that in those circumstances Austria will not have any need to join NATO: it will enjoy NATO protection without membership. But taking a free ride would reduce Austria, in terms of security, to an object of NATO policy. "A seat at the table" will be necessary to preserve an independent role.

For Finland, an Austrian decision to apply for NATO membership would not by itself have a domino effect. As in the case of EU membership, Swedish policy will be decisive. When I predicted in my speech that Sweden would go first and pull Finland with it into NATO, I was met with incredulity in both countries. Surely, it was said, Sweden would be the last country to join a military alliance. True, it has kept out of wars since 1815. But the popular image of Sweden as the perennial neutral stems from a superficial view of the character of Swedish policy. Sweden has not been neutral in the sense of sitting on the fence, like Switzerland. Sweden has kept out of military alliances in order to preserve its freedom of action in international affairs. It has never been a passive onlooker.

Olof Palme dramatically demonstrated the Swedish will to influence international politics. In his time, the European situation was frozen, leaving no scope for an active role for Sweden, but Palme found one in the Third World. Today, the action is in Europe. But in this age of integration, a country can exert influence only within the international institutions—in this case, the European Union and NATO. Once Poland has become a member of NATO and after some years of the EU, the relative influence of Sweden and Finland on issues related to Russia, the Baltic states, and European security in general will be considerably reduced. Will Sweden resign itself to a secondary role?

Carl Bildt, the chairman of the leading opposition party, the Moderate Conservatives, has already given his answer: His party has declared that Sweden should consider joining the New NATO. The Social Democratic government is not prepared to go that far. The party is divided on EMU, even on the EU itself, and the government depends in Parliament on the support of the Center Party, which is opposed to any further integration. But the government has joined Finland's example by telling NATO that its present policy is subject to revision in the event of a change in the European situation. What in May 1996 was unthinkable became a possible alternative in 1997.

Although Finland and Sweden now appear to move in step on security issues, the geopolitical divide has not disappeared. Unlike the Finns, the Swedes do not look upon their membership in the EU as an insurance against isolation in an international crisis. A majority of Swedes still believe that isolation—meaning neutrality—is not the problem but the solution. They can afford to be more relaxed about their country's relations with NATO. To join or not to join is not a life-and-death question: either way there will still be Finland between Sweden and Russia.

In Finland, until quite recently, security policy has been based on an ideology of self-reliance, rather than neutrality in the accepted sense of that term: self-reliance not just as something imposed by unkind fate, but as a source of patriotic pride, the best alternative chosen by the nation itself. Conscription remains an indispensable element. Almost 90 percent of all the males of service age enter the armed forces and more than 80 percent complete their training. The number of conscientious objectors is the lowest in Western democracies. This attests to the continued will of the Finnish people to defend themselves. Opinion surveys show that people trust the defense forces more than any other public institution. Conscription enables Finland to maintain large reserves, and in time of crisis 430,000 troops can be mobilized for territorial defense.

According to the Finnish defense doctrine, a possible aggressor will always have superior forces at his disposal. He cannot be stopped at the border or any other fixed line. He can be defeated only by delaying and wearing him down in the whole depth of the country. Ground forces play a central role. Their weapons and equipment cannot be of the same standard as in professional armies, but they have been designed for the Finnish terrain, climate, and conditions, and they are suitable to be handled by citizens in uniform. The navy is small but modern, with an average ship age of only nine years. The air force is in process of deploying 64 F/A18 Hornets. And the Finnish government refuses to give up land mines, which form an integral part of the country's defense system.

Ask a Finnish general who is the enemy, and, without blinking an eyelid, he will tell you that Finland has no enemies. He will explain that there is no reason to assume that Finland might be attacked for its own sake, in an isolated action. But the country could be drawn into a wider European conflict. An invader might try to pass through Finland on his way to somewhere else, or he might wish to prevent others from using Finnish territory. No names are named.

Officially, Finland continues to maintain an independent national defense, but in fact the doctrine of self-reliance has been substantially modified. Finland now cooperates with NATO on a broad front. It joined the Partnership for Peace program in May 1994, the NATO planning and review process in February 1995, and has participated in the Bosnian operations, IFOR and SFOR, from their beginning. It has sent officers to work in the PfP staff elements established in NATO commands, all the way from SHAPE to subregional headquarters. Since May 1996 Finland has carried on what is called an intensified dialogue with NATO, and it became a member of the Euro-Atlantic Partnership Council at its inception. A Finnish diplomatic mission to NATO has been established.

On a more material level, the Finnish government's White

Paper on defense issued in March 1997 strongly advocates the development of "interoperability" in support of international crisis management. In plain language this means the adoption by the Finnish defense forces of NATO standards and procedures. Of the fully mobilized defense forces, 3 of the 23 brigades will be equipped as Rapid Deployment Brigades, and 1 of the 3 will be specially earmarked for international crisis management tasks and trained and equipped accordingly. It will be fully operational by the year 2000. Interoperability, the White Paper says, indirectly improves Finland's own defense, because it facilitates the reception of outside assistance in a situation in which the country's own resources prove to be insufficient: self-reliance finally has its limits.[16]

In the words of former U.S. ambassador to NATO Robert Hunter, NATO will seek to reinvigorate the Partnership for Peace program so that "we make the difference between being a partner and being an ally razor thin." Such a close relationship with NATO means giving up the advantage of neutrality or nonalignment in a future crisis without getting the security guarantee of Article 5 of the North Atlantic Treaty in return. Why then stop short of crossing that thin line?

An explanation was given by President Martti Ahtisaari in a speech on June 3, 1997, at the Assembly of the Western European Union: "By being fully integrated into the European Union but by remaining militarily non-allied, we contribute to a controlled process of change with maximum stability in the Northern part of our continent." This convoluted language intends to say that by not seeking NATO membership, Finland avoids provoking Russia into adopting policies that might make it more difficult to bring the Baltic states into the EU, if not NATO. This line of thinking recalls the Cold War concept of the "Nordic balance," according to which the neutrality of Sweden and the self-imposed restraints of Norway's role within NATO helped Finland maintain its independence. Today, it is argued, a similar restraint on the part of Finland and Sweden helps the Baltic states. This view implies that Old NATO and Old Russia still confront each other in the Baltic region and that Finnish and Swedish restraint has a moderating influence on Russia. But now that NATO and Russia have joined forces in defense of European stability, Finland and Sweden face a more complex problem. They will have to consider the possible consequences of NATO-Russia cooperation, as well as those of a possible confrontation. Decisions on security in the Baltic region may be taken over their heads by the NATO-Russia Council. And because NATO has become the security arm of the European Union, Finland and Sweden will find themselves second-class members in Brussels as well. In fact, as both NATO and the EU expand, the two concepts of security are bound to merge, leading to a congruence between the membership of the two institutions.

But politics remain stuck in old grooves. In the absence of an external threat or pressure, politicians tend to put off dealing with controversial issues. The present coalition government, whose mandate runs until March 1999, is focused on getting Finland into EMU, an objective that puts a great deal of strain on its inner cohesion. It is not likely to burden its agenda with another divisive issue. Public opinion supports the government position. Polls indicate that people are in favor of maintaining the NATO option, but on membership 60 percent are opposed and only 20 percent in favor. It must be asked, however, which NATO those interviewed have in mind—the New or the Old? In public perceptions, New NATO and New Russia are cardboard figures, not reality. Finnish opinion on national security is likely to be affected less by sophisticated arguments about influence in the decision-making process than by what will happen in Russia.

# 6

# Russia

Finns view Russia through a prism reflecting centuries of inter-action between the two peoples. None can credibly claim to be detached in the sense of being unaffected by history and, in many cases, by personal experiences. Each generation has had its own vision of the neighbor. My parents knew, and valued, St. Petersburg as a great European cultural center, before it was closed down by the Bolshevik revolution. The history I was taught at school in the 1930s made me look upon Russia, Czarist or Communist, as the permanent enemy of Finland's freedom—a view brutally confirmed by the Soviet invasion in 1939. But after the war, we who had fought and survived learned that it was, after all, possible for an independent Finland to live with the ebb and flow of Russian imperial power. My children, who reached adulthood in the late 1970s, came to take this for granted; in their eyes, the Soviet Union remained a menace because of its military power, but as a society it was stagnant and uninteresting.

Today, the menace in the old sense has faded away. The Russian state is so weak that it is incapable of collecting the taxes due to it, with the result that it can neither pay its civil servants on time nor feed its soldiers. The center is losing control to various units of the federal system. Laws and decrees issued from Moscow are often flouted by local authorities. Organized crime and corrup-tion further erode the government's authority.

The very weakness of the Russian state generates a new set of risks for its neighbors. Unsafe nuclear power plants are in opera-tion just across Finland's eastern border. Sewage from St. Petersburg is polluting the waters of the Gulf of Finland, and poisonous clouds drift westward from antiquated industrial plants in the Kola peninsula. Russian criminal gangs operate across the border, bringing drugs and prostitutes in their wake.

To dwell on such risks is to approach Russia through the back entrance where the garbage piles up. A more balanced vision is needed. When told that Russia is weak, many Finns respond with cautionary tales from the past. Russia has been weak before, but has always risen to strength again: surely we must be prepared for this to happen once more.

There is no consensus on the future of Russia among the many Finns who have intimate knowledge of the country, as scholars, businessmen, or journalists. But on the whole, Finns are inclined to stress the continuity in Russian developments. Richard Pipes has pointed out that even the Bolshevik revolution could not have caused a complete transformation of the thousand-year-old history of a vast and populous country: "The same people, habiting the same territory, speaking the same language, held to a common past, could hardly have been fashioned into different creatures by a sudden change of government."[1] The same can be said of the abrupt change that took place on the last day of 1991. True, the Soviet Union is dead, but it is only brain-dead; the organs of the old system continue to function. The revolution that put an end to the Soviet Union as a state was like a neutron bomb in reverse: it destroyed the structures without removing the people in power. The great majority of the men—there are very few women among them—who run Russia today belonged to the former Soviet *nomenklatura*. The switch from one system to another has hardly caused them severe pangs of conscience because for most of them the Soviet ideology was a mere facade for the exercise of power: democracy serves the same purpose.

The case of the first Russian ambassador to Finland, Yuri Deryabin, is revealing. In a book of memoirs published in Finnish at the end of his term in 1995, he describes his earlier career as an official in the Soviet foreign service specializing in Finland and the other Nordic countries. He was by his own account an active member of the Communist Party—no closet dissident. In 1992, however, upon receiving his appointment from President Yeltsin to become ambassador to Finland, Deryabin saw the light. Before leaving for Helsinki, he called on Patriarch Aleksei for guidance, and shortly afterward he was baptized by an Orthodox priest in Helsinki. He became a devout churchgoer. Yet Deryabin declares: "I was not a turncoat." The statement is not so absurd as it may seem at first glance. From the beginning of his working life, Deryabin has been a loyal servant of the state. Until the end of 1991, it was the Soviet Union; now it is the Russian Federation. The state, not Deryabin, is the turncoat. He remains loyal to Russia, whatever its form of government is called. And he is no exception among the members of the vast former Soviet bureaucracy.

One's view of Russia's future depends ultimately on whether or not one believes in the Enlightenment concept of a universal model of development—an irreversible march toward democracy and market economy. The majority of the Russian elite rejects the validity of such a model. President Yeltsin himself has said that Russia is different, that the national character of the Russian people is not like that of other Europeans—which to Finns sounds like a statement of the obvious. The Slavophile vision of Russians as a people apart—a people with superior spiritual values and with a world mission—still inspires many Russians. But one could also argue that, on the contrary, Russia is no different from other nations. No country has ever been able to acquire a system of parliamentary democracy and market economy off the peg, as it were, like buying a ready-made suit. Everywhere it has required a long evolutionary process. In Russia such an evolution has hardly begun.

Russia does have one foot in the open market, but the other foot is stuck under the heavy weight of old structures. The country is straddling two worlds, shifting its weight from one foot to the other in response to conflicting pressures, external and internal.

How to define its present character is a matter of endless debate among Russians themselves. The fact that for the first time in history the head of state as well as the members of the legislature, the state Duma, have been elected in free elections does not, by itself, make Russia a democracy. The political parties have not yet taken root among the people; paradoxically, the Communists, the enemies of democracy, are the only party with a functioning nationwide organization. The president rules in authoritarian fashion, with the Duma playing mainly an obstructionist role. The media are controlled by an oligarchy of financial barons whose immense wealth and extensive control of the media make them a kind of shadow government. According to George Soros, "Russia today is a parody of an open society."[2]

The West has showered upon the Russians good advice on

how to solve their economic problems, but no outsider can help them to tackle the root cause of their present misery—the collapse of public morality. Macroeconomic indicators may be pointing upward, but they do not measure the extent of criminal activity and corruption, the decay of the social infrastructure, the consequences of ecological neglect, or the depth of despair and cynicism among the Russian population.

For Finland and other neighboring countries, the crucial question is how Russia will deal with its postimperial identity crisis. The phenomenon itself is of course familiar to students of the rise and fall of great powers. The British and the French, too, have had difficulties in reconciling themselves to the loss of empire. But in some respects the Russian case is unique. While the British and the French had to withdraw from overseas possessions populated by alien peoples, the Russian domain itself has shrunk in size, leaving 25 million Russians outside the Russian Federation, beyond borders that used to be merely administrative divisions. What makes this contraction all the more painful is that the Russians, again unlike the British and the French, have no established national or geographical identity to fall back on. What is Russia if not an empire?

Actually the Russian withdrawal from the "inner empire" is more apparent than real. The former Soviet republics belonging to the Commonwealth of Independent States (CIS) remain chained to Russia by the structures of the former Soviet military-industrial complex; most of their leaders are members of the *nomenklatura*, and the Russian Army has intervened in conflicts in Moldova, as well as along the southern rim of the former Soviet Union where a new "Great Game" for the control of the oil and gas resources of the Caspian Sea is now under way.

Is Russian domination within the CIS a form of imperialism that has to be resisted before it advances even further, or is it a natural and inevitable consequence of the interdependence between the members of the CIS—a process of "reintegration," as the Russians themselves prefer to call it?

The question presents Western policymakers with a dilemma they would prefer not to face. It was never an objective of Western policy to bring about the disintegration of the Soviet Union. Yet, once the Soviet Union had fallen apart, the West rushed to recognize the former Soviet republics as sovereign states and to admit them to international organizations. Ironically, what Stalin proposed in

1945 has now come to pass: all 15 former Soviet republics have been granted a vote in the UN. As in the case of Yugoslavia, the principle of national self-determination was applied indiscriminately, on demand, without an examination of the credentials of each applicant. Clearly, some of them would not pass any reasonable test of viable statehood. The consequences may be as tragic as has been the breakdown of the former African colonies that were turned into "instant states" in the 1960s.

The aspirations of the Russian elite to "reintegrate" the countries of the CIS—to put the Soviet Union (minus the Baltics) together again—are bound to run into economic difficulties. The fate of the attempt to create a "union" between Russian and Belarus is a case in point. Belarus, with its population of 10 million, seemed well suited to be the first CIS member to return to the fold. It has no strong national or linguistic identity of its own; its statehood is in fact an artificial construction. Yet the union agreement signed in April 1997 by presidents Yeltsin and Lukashenka was gutted by the Russian government of all substance, partly because the dictatorial system in Belarus did not suit the Moscow reformers, but also because the economy of Belarus is in even worse shape than that of Russia.

This will not, however, be the last word on the subject of "reintegration." Russia's limited capabilities will not deter Moscow from pursuing the goal of restoring its role as a great power. Russian policy, according to Foreign Minister Yevgeniy Primakov, is carried out, not on the basis of current weakness, but on the basis of Russia's "colossal potential."[3]

The shape and character of the New Russia expected to rise out of the ruins of the Soviet system remain hazy. President Yeltsin has set up a commission of wise men to define what might be the "Russian idea" in the twenty-first century. In the meantime we know what Americans want it to be. Deputy secretary of state Strobe Talbott has said that the U.S. goal, "like that of many Russians, is to see Russia become a normal, modern state—democratic in its governments, abiding by its own constitution and by its own laws, market-orientated and prosperous in its economic development, in peace with itself and the rest of the world"[4]—in other words, a country like the United States. Would the New Russia then also have its own Monroe Doctrine and the capacity to project military power beyond its own borders to protect its far-flung interests?

The views on Russia's future expressed in my *International*

*Herald Tribune* columns (and now in this book) have elicited a critical reaction from an American friend, one of the world's great authorities on Russia. The essence of George Kennan's letter (dated November 15, 1996) is contained in the following paragraphs:

I doubt that there would be any serious inclination on the part of either the people or the present government in Russia to go in for any form of imperialistic expansion either in the West or along its other borders. There are, to be sure, spots in the postwar status quo where borders were so poorly drawn in the immediate postwar period or at the time of the demise of the Soviet Union that they positively invite trouble. The former East Prussia and the Crimea are examples. It will take a great deal of patience and constructive imagination to find better solutions to those particular problems. But I have seen no signs of any disposition on anybody's part in Moscow to try to solve them in the foreseeable future by military action.

What surprises and disturbs me about the pessimistic distrust of Russia which, it seems to me, is reflected . . . in some writings . . . here in this country, is that they appear to identify the present Russian regime with the Communist one that preceded it, as though the changes of the past eight years had no significance in this respect . . . as though the behavior of Stalin and his successors was merely one more reflection of an unchanging thirst for territorial expansion on the part (by implication) of an incurably bloody-minded Russian population.

How far removed is this from the realities of the present day! This *fin de siècle* Russia, as I am sure you know much better than do many others, is a dreadfully injured country . . . injured spiritually, genetically, socially and politically by seven decades (three generations) of Communist power and by other vicissitudes of this terrible and brutal century, including outstandingly the Second World War. It is a shadow of its former self.

This is not the fault of the mass of the Russian people . . . rather, of the discipline exerted upon them by the surrounding circumstances of their lives. They were the first victims, not the authors, of the Communist oppression and aggression of which so many of the rest of you were also the sufferers. While of course the crisis in their life is not over, the extraordinary bloodlessness of the great revolution that has taken place in their country in the last five to six years seems to me to speak for their humanity rather than for any innately aggressive inclinations.

The present Russian regime is of course in many respects a pathetic one. It is only five or six years old. What more could have been expected from it? Its Communist past left few human resources from which a new and wise leadership could be recruited.

But is all this adequate reason for saddling this regime and all that it represents with expectations and assumptions that reflect only the worst memories of the past? Should we not allow it more time to show what sort of a force it can be in world affairs in the years to come? Should we not, in other words, give it a chance?

I wrote in my reply that I was not one of those who have been criticized for believing that aggressiveness is somehow imprinted in the genetic code of the Russian people. I do believe that Russia can, and most probably, will change. I have seen in my lifetime how Finland has changed. More important, I believe Germany has undergone a fundamental change. It has rejected militarism, irrevocably. I do not agree with Hegel who wrote that "what experience and history teach us is this—that people and governments never have learned anything from history, or acted on principles reduced from it." Hegel's philosophy had a profound influence on Germany, but now the Germans have shown by their actions that he was wrong. But they learned the hard way. The country was defeated, divided, occupied, and denazified. Its former leaders were hanged as criminals.

Russia, however, has not settled its accounts with the past. The majority of the people who run the country today were members of the Soviet ruling elite. Many Russians seem genuinely to believe that they had been betrayed by Gorbachev in collusion with the West. They have not turned their backs on Stalin and his regime. Lenin's body remains on view in the mausoleum on Red Square. The present chaos generates nostalgia for the past, even among people who are firmly opposed to the Soviet system. I do not belittle the importance of the change that has taken place, and I am not predicting a return to totalitarian rule. Indeed, a centralized dictatorship can hardly be imposed in this information age. More chaos may well be a greater danger.

Of course we must give Russia a chance: Is this not what Western policy is all about? Let us hope Russia will gradually evolve into a stable society with a strong economic interest in maintaining peaceful relations with its neighbors. But this may take a generation or two.

A landscape changes its shape and color depending on the point from which it is observed. My American friend can see Russia from the height of his accumulated knowledge and experience as a vast panorama stretching out at his feet. My view of Russia is from the foot of a steep and formidable mountain that casts its shadow over where I stand. Time, too, means different things to different people. To a historian, one or two generations is a relatively short period. To all except the very young, it means "not in our lifetime."

The Finnish people will have to deal as best they can with whatever regime that may come into power in the vast country next door. Even in the worst case, Finland's position will be less vulnerable than at any previous time during the twentieth century. For Russia, Finland now is a more useful partner, both politically and economically, than in the past. Within the European Union, Finland will always work, in its own interest, for good relations with Russia, and now that the cloud of Finlandization has been dispelled, Finland's views on Russia are listened to in Brussels. Such a rational view of Russia's interests is gaining ground in Moscow. Only the extreme neo-imperialists still look upon Finland as part of their patrimony. For their part, today's Finns are on the whole remarkably free of resentments or hang-ups in their attitude toward Russia—self-confident without vindictiveness.

On the ground, the border crossings between Finland and Russia are now jammed with traffic. Trade is bouncing back after its collapse at the beginning of the decade. In 1996 and 1997, Finnish exports to Russia grew by 25 percent annually, rising to about 7 percent of Finland's total exports. But the character of Finnish-Russian trade has changed radically. Instead of the few large companies that used to dominate Finnish exports to the Soviet Union, hundreds of small and medium-sized enterprises now do business with Russia. The assortment of goods Finland is now selling is also different from what it used to be. It does not include investment goods, ships, and other products that need export credits. Because Russia cannot cover the risk, the trade is now cash-and-carry, and at least half of the goods are paid for in advance. Russian magazines and books printed on presses in Finland are the number-one export item. Mobile phones, paint, shoes, food products, and other consumer goods are being sold in the Russian market. Finland has also established itself as a transit center for Russian trade to and from the rest of the world and is making efforts to become a base for foreign companies trading with Russia.

There are, however, many barriers to a further expansion of Finnish-Russian trade. Finnish businessmen are frustrated by bureaucratic interference, long hold-ups for trucks at border crossings, constantly changing tax rules, and rampant corruption by Russian officials. The lack of export financing is the main obstacle to a return of large-scale capital projects Finland used to supply to the Soviet Union. As long as wealthy Russians prefer to send their money abroad it is difficult to persuade Finnish companies to invest in Russia.

Finnish imports from Russia—about 6 percent of all imports in 1997—still consist mainly of oil and gas as in the Soviet days, but a new element is the money spent by Russian tourists. In spite of visa requirements, more than 700,000 Russian visitors crossed the border into Finland in 1997. The small Finnish border town of Lappeenranta is flourishing, thanks to a steady flow of well-off Russians from St. Petersburg who regularly drive the distance of 290 kilometers to do their shopping on the Finnish side of the border.

Contrary to expectations, the metropolitan area of St. Petersburg has not become the main market for Finnish exports. In the Soviet period, its economy was heavily dominated by military industries that are now being severely reduced, and effort to develop alternative productions have been disappointing so far. But St. Petersburg is slowly regaining its role as a cultural center. The projected high-speed rail link between Helsinki and St. Petersburg, to be financed partly by loans from the European Union, is expected to boost the city's development. Its port facilities also need improvement.

Grants, loans, and investments from various EU programs, the European Investment Bank, the European Bank for Reconstruction and Development, the U.S. government, and other U.S. institutions as well as from private companies now flow into the Baltic region, including northwestern Russia, part of it channeled through Finland. The amounts are not so spectacular as to attract media attention, but the total effect is nonetheless a significant contribution to modernizing the infrastructure in Russia and the Baltic states, creating cross-border links between them, and supporting market-oriented economic activities. A number of governmental and non-governmental organizations are working to strengthen democratic institutions and entrepreneurship in the former Communist countries. Improving nuclear safety is another important goal of cooperation. Among U.S. organizations active in the region, the Center for Strategic and International Studies (CSIS) is focusing attention on security issues. On the top level, the prime ministers of all the Baltic Sea countries, including Russia, participate in the meetings of the Council of the Baltic Sea States.

This jumble of partly overlapping organizations, programs, projects, and schemes is a kind of mini-Marshall plan designed to create security and stability through political cooperation and economic integration in the Baltic region. Will this "soft" activity be enough without the backing of the hard shield of NATO? Pessimists warn that "things fall apart, the center cannot hold." But young people in Russia are grasping at the opportunities offered by an open society. It is a race against time.

# Conclusion

In the latter half of year 1999 from July 1 to December 31, it will be Finland's turn to hold the rotating presidency of the European Union. Several hundred meetings of various EU bodies will be held during that period in different locations in Finland, including the northernmost town on the Arctic Circle. In mid-December, the meetings will culminate in a gathering in Helsinki of the 15 heads of state or government under the chairmanship of the Finnish president—the last summit of the twentieth century. Altogether around 20,000 persons from other European countries—politicians, officials, experts, journalists—are expected to visit Finland during those six months, many of them probably for the first time. Finland will no longer be "a nation that dwells alone."

To Finns, the presidency will have a powerful symbolic meaning. It will be exactly 100 years since the Russian emperor issued his edict restricting Finnish self-rule, an act that at the time was believed to spell the end of Finland as a nation, but in fact was the beginning of the Finnish national struggle for an independent existence that has been carried on by a variety of means and at different levels of intensity ever since. Membership in the EU has finally provided Finland with a secure place among the independent states of Europe.

The conclusion may seem paradoxical: surely membership in the EU restricts Finnish sovereignty. But the sovereignty of small states like Finland has always been circumscribed by the realities of power. Membership in the EU grants them an influence, or at least the right to be heard they have not had before.

The presidency will be a great show that will surely lift the spirits of the Finnish people. But it would be wrong to imagine that Finns go about their daily business feeling proud of the great gains their country has made during the twentieth century. The claim I make in the introduction of this book—that Finland has emerged as a winner from the ordeals of the past 100 years—may well be dismissed by many of my compatriots as hollow. They may argue that it is not such a great achievement to win a medal in a race in which most of the competitors have fallen by the wayside because of injuries or been disqualified for cheating. Rather than looking back, they are peering anxiously ahead wondering what may be in store for them in the twenty-first century.

Not so long ago the answer would have been presented in the form of scenarios that would consist of three pillars: the first painting a picture of the future too good to be true and the second too horrible to contemplate, so we would plump for the third, which predicted partly cloudy weather with occasional showers and variable winds. But no scenario predicted the fall of the Berlin Wall, and since 1989 political scenarios have been out of fashion. Instead, forecasters have borrowed from modern physics the uncertainty principle: because random change is possible, the future is simply unpredictable. The only certainty is that change will continue.

With Europe in a state of flux, the future of Finland will depend on its ability to adjust to changing conditions. In this respect Finland has a number of important assets. It is a homogeneous, well-functioning, orderly society, with a civil service that overall is competent and efficient. Corruption is incidental, not endemic. The gap between income groups is narrower than in most other EU countries, which makes Finland an egalitarian society with a high degree of cohesion. As much as 14 percent of the government budget is spent on public education: this too contributes to social equality. The political system is stable. As the record shows, Finns are pragmatic people, not prone to fanaticism. Traditional civic virtues are still respected, and the Protestant work ethic prevails, though crumbling around the edges.

Industry and business are adjusting to changing conditions. Mergers are producing units large enough to compete successfully in the global markets. In the forest industry, for instance, the former field of a dozen or more companies has been reduced to three giants, one of which (UPM-Kymmene) is now the biggest producer of paper and board in Europe and the second biggest in the world.

This points to a dilemma faced by small nations in this age of integration. Is a corporation big enough to be successful in the global market too big for Finland? UPM-Kymmene accounts for as much as 13 percent of Finland's total earnings of foreign currencies. There is an obvious danger in such a heavy dependence on one private company.

The challenge to national independence posed by the globalization of business will remain a sensitive issue. In Sweden, this was illustrated by the uproar caused by a May 1997 statement from L.M. Ericsson, manufacturer of telecommunications equipment. Its CEO warned the Swedish government that the company might have to move its headquarters to another country because heavy taxation makes it impossible to recruit foreign staff for work in Sweden. He pointed out that Ericsson does not need Sweden, but Sweden needs the $7 billion of export income earned by the company.

The head of Ericsson's Finnish competitor, Nokia, had a different view, however. Mr. Jorma Ollila stated that Finland remained important for Nokia: "The people, the atmosphere, the education and the basic economic policies are right. Nokia's corporate culture, its underlying ethos and the strength of its product development are Finnish."[1] Although Finland accounts for only 6 percent of Nokia's total sales, more than 55 percent of its total products are made in Finland, more than 50 percent of its total workforce are in Finland, and 78 percent of its development staff are in this country. Since Nokia's share in Finland's total exports in 1997 is 15 percent, the national credo of Nokia's management has a profound political significance.

Nokia today ranks number two behind Motorola in overall mobile handset sales, but is the world leader in digital phones, which are now displacing the first generation of analogue phones, while Ericsson claims to be the world's largest supplier of telephone equipment. How is it possible that these two companies based in Nordic welfare states with high wages now share the commanding heights of the global mobile phone industry? *Time* magazine offered an answer in its July 14, 1997, issue. The Nordic countries, according to *Time*, got a head start in 1981 by launching the world's pioneering international cellular phone network, the Nordic Mobile Telephone system (NMT). But this is a superficial explanation. Why were they able to get a head start? The answer is in the qualities of life mentioned by the Nokia chief. This proves that high-wage, social-welfare European countries can maintain their competitive edge on a high technological level. According to an OECD study, unit labor costs in high-tech industries in Finland have actually declined because very strong productivity growth has compensated for nominal wage increases.[2] This explains, partly, why unemployment remains high while the economy is growing at a rate of 4 percent a year. It also points to the solution of this problem: education—a slow process.

The tax issue remains of crucial importance. High marginal tax, rising above 60 percent, hits the minority of Finns who by virtue of education and language skills are able to take advantage of the opportunities offered by the Common Market. Finland cannot afford a debilitating brain drain. But the demand for tax relief for higher income groups clashes with the egalitarian ideology behind the progressive tax systems in the Nordic countries. The government is determined to balance its budget by the year 2000 and then begin to reduce public debt. Substantial tax reductions can only be achieved through cuts in spending. This, too, will be a slow process.

Adapting to change requires becoming more like other countries. Every turn of the integrationist screw reduces distinctions. How far will this go? In an article devoted to the fiftieth anniversary of the Marshall Plan, OECD secretary-general Donald Johnston quoted the words of Canadian poet Frank Scott: "The world is my country, the human race my race." Johnston added: "When that becomes a conviction of all mankind, the Marshall vision will have been fulfilled."[3] A terrifying vision—mankind homogenized.

So once again the Finns are told the end is near. This time it is not rape by Russian imperialism that is expected to put an end to the independence of Finland: the new enemy is globalization. In this view, the global technostructure of finance and industry will finally render the nation-state obsolete. The best and the brightest will drift to the great financial centers, perhaps keeping a summer cottage on a lake somewhere in Finland, while those left behind will lack the intellectual resources needed to maintain a distinct cultural identity. They will cease to be a nation; they will become a group of producers and consumers living in one corner of the Common Market.

The threat to national identity posed by economic integration is perceived in countries much bigger and more powerful than Finland. It has been graphically described by a French politician of the Left, Jean-Pierre Chevènement, who wrote in 1980 that if things went on as they were, by the year 2000 France would be a kind of Algeria appended to the United States, with the majority of the French, in berets, their liter of red wine and their Camembert in their pouches, continuing to speak French in mountain villages. One more scenario that has failed to materialize.[4]

Obviously, economic integration creates an ever greater interdependence between states, and this inevitably reduces the scope of independent action. Every nation chafes from time to time under the constraints imposed upon it, while the advantages gained through economic integration are taken for granted. Yet the independence of Finland, measured by the capacity of its government to safeguard and promote the interests of its citizens, is surely now far greater than it was at the time when the country was poor, backward, and wholly dependent upon the export of forest products. As a small country, Finland has little influence on the general trends of the world economy, but within the frames set by those trends, success or failure depends on its own performance—its ability to maximize the benefits of integration and minimize its negative effects. National independence has become a function of economic competitiveness.

This view is rejected by the Greens and other seekers of alternative life styles who believe the industrial world is heading toward a general breakdown. Why should Finland compete so strenuously for a first-class passage on a ship that is bound to sink soon? They advocate the reduction of Finland's dependence on the world economy through a return to a simpler way of life that would save the natural environment from further destruction. Such a retreat from the evil world into the security of an inner citadel has been the dream of stoics and ascetics, religious leaders, and revolutionary philosophers throughout the ages. It sounds vaguely appealing to those who long for some respite from the strains of competitive living, but its adherents remain a fringe group in Finland and elsewhere in Europe.

True, the global industrial technostructure not only obliterates the animal and vegetable diversity of our planet but endangers human diversity as well. The number of languages in the world is shrinking: of the roughly 6,500 languages now spoken, up to half are already endangered or on the brink of distinction. Linguists estimate that a language dies somewhere every two weeks. According to one expert, the world stands to lose up to 95 percent of all its languages in the coming century.[5]

The death of a language is fatal to national identity. The British writer and historian Jan Morris has written a heart-rending obituary on the loss of the Welsh language—"a treasure of Europe, with its own wonderful structure of literature, tradition, myth and legend, but also a lively, flexible, everyday working tongue." The pressures of integration, Morris wrote, threatening the national personality of Wales had been intensified beyond resistance.[6]

Had Finland remained part of Sweden, Finnish may never have been developed into a language of culture. But under Russian rule the Finnish language flourished, and attempts at russification were successfully resisted. As an imperial power, Russia failed to exercise the kind of cultural influence that Britain and France had among their subject peoples. This is also shown by the survival of the Estonian language after 50 years of repression by the Soviets. There are no rules: some languages and nations succumb to the pressures of integration and unification; others do not.

The Finnish language is now safely ensconced as one of the 11 official languages of the European Union. To permit representatives of each member state to use their own language is a cumbersome way of doing business: 33 interpreters are needed to translate 110 language combinations at a single meeting. In practice English, French, and German are used as working languages. But to strike the language of a member state from the list of official languages would be an affront to the independence of that state: language makes the nation.

Has Finland now reached the point in history when the absence of external threat begins to undermine internal cohesion and weaken the sense of national purpose? There are as yet no obvious symptoms of this widespread post-Cold War infection. As newcomers to the European Union, Finns feel they have to prove themselves as a serious partner. They retain a competitive attitude to international relations. And there is always the Big Neighbor. Unlike some other small nations living in safer and more comfortable environments, the Finnish people will not lack the stimulus of external challenges. It will keep the Finnish national spirit alive.

# Notes

## Introduction

1. The phrase was used by Harold Macmillan during a visit to Helsinki on June 6, 1979, when he recalled his first visit to Finland as a member of a British parliamentary delegation during the Winter War of 1940. At the time, the whole Western world admired the Finnish resistance to the Soviet invasion, after which admiration turned into pity for the small nation abandoned by the democracies. Macmillan went on to predict that Finland could well become the object of envy once its success in maintaining its way of life became better known.

2. Eric Hobsbawm, *The Age of Extreme: The Short Twentieth Century, 1914–1991* (London: Michael Joseph, 1994), 111. The other countries that made Hobsbawm's list were Britain, the Irish Free State, Sweden, and Switzerland.

3. This was proclaimed in November 1990 in the Charter of Paris issued by the summit meeting of the Conference on Security and Cooperation in Europe.

4. Milan Kundera, "The Tragedy of Central Europe," *New York Review of Books*, April 26, 1994.

5. Isaac Deutscher, *Stalin: A Political Biography* (London: Oxford University Press, 1949), 124.

6. J. W. Snellman, *Näin Puhui Snellman* [Thus spoke Snellman] (Helsinki: WSOY, 1960).

7. Fernand Braudel, *A History of Civilizations* (New York: Penguin Books, 1995), 531.

## Chapter 1

1. Karin von Hippel, "The Resurgence of Nationalism and Its International Implications," *Washington Quarterly* 17, no. 4 (Fall 1994): 185.

2. Daniel Patrick Moynihan, *Pandemonium: Ethnicity in International Politics* (New York: Oxford University Press, 1993).

3. Charles Krauthammer, "Sane, Reliable Canada Attempts Suicide—and Will Do So Again," *International Herald Tribune*, November 4, 1995.

4. Solzhenitsyn's comment quoted in the Finnish monthly *Kanava*, no. 4 (1996).

5. "Two Concepts of Nationalism: An Interview with Isaiah Berlin." *New York Review of Books*, November 21, 1991.

6. Anthony Powell, *Venusberg* (London: Penguin Books, 1961), 65.

7. See Max Jakobson, *Finnish Neutrality* (London: Hugh Evelyn, 1968), 7–10.

## Chapter 2

1. *Documents of British Foreign Policy, 1919–1939*, Series III, Band V (London: HMSO, 1952), 228–229, 668–669.

2. Max Jakobson, *The Diplomacy of the Winter War* (Cambridge: Harvard University Press, 1961), 105–154, contains a detailed account of the Finnish-Soviet talks in October-November 1939.

3. Ibid., 117.

4. Jakobson, *Finnish Neutrality*, 16–17.

5. Fred Iklé, *Every War Must End* (New York: Columbia University Press, 1971).

6. Dmitri Volkogonov, *Stalin: Triumph and Tragedy* (London: Weidenfeld and Nicolson, 1991), 359.

7. From an interview with President Meri, which is included in a Finnish language collection of his speeches, *Tulen Maasta Jonka Nimi on Viro* [I come from a country called Estonia] (Helsinki: Otava, 1995).

8. Timothy Garton Ash, "Hungary's Revolution: Forty Years On," *New York Review of Books*, November 14, 1996.

9. See "Soviet-Finnish War" in *Bol'shaya Sovetskaya Entsiklopediya* [Great Soviet encyclopedia], ed. A. M. Prokhorov (New York: Macmillan, 1973).

10. See David L. Williams, "The Fate of the Frozen History of the Winter War," paper prepared for the 104th annual meeting of the American Historical Association, December 27–30, 1989.

11. Volkogonov, *Stalin*, 365.

12. Winston S. Churchill, *The Second World War*, vol. 7, *Triumph & Tragedy* (London: Cassell, 1954), 317–318.

13. Volkogonov, *Stalin*, 365–366.

14. Charles E. Bohlen, *Witness to History, 1929–1969* (New York: Norton, 1973), 150–151.

15. Milovan Djilas, *Conversations with Stalin* (New York: Harcourt, Brace & World, 1962), 114.

## Chapter 3

1. Zbigniew Brzezinski, *Game Plan* (Boston: The Atlantic Monthly Press, 1986), 89.

2. President Paasikivi's diaries of the years 1944–1956 were published by WSOY Publishing Company, Helsinki, in full in two volumes in 1985–1986 (*J.K. Paasikiven Paivakirjat 1944–1956* [The diaries of J.K. Paasikivi 1944–1956], Yrjo Blomstedt and Matti Klinge, eds.). An edited Swedish version has also been published.

3. Alan Bullock, *Ernest Bevin, Foreign Secretary, 1945–1951* (New York, London: W.W. Norton & Company, 1983), 513–525.

4. Jakobson, *Finnish Neutrality*, 40–44.

5. Andrei Zdanov's diary of the years he served as the head of the Allied Control Commission in Helsinki has been made available to Finnish scholars at the Archives of the Soviet Communist Party.

6. Feliks I. Chuev, *Molotov Remembers: Inside Kremlin Politics; Conversations with Feliks Chuev*, edited with an introduction and notes by Albert Resis (Chicago: Ivan R. Dee, 1993), 10.

7. Margaret Thatcher, *The Downing Street Years* (New York: Harper Collins, 1993), 10. (First earl of Chatham William Pitt was an eighteenth century British statesman and prime minister, 1766–1768.)

8. Niccolo Machiavelli, *The Prince*, chapter 21 (many editions).

9. Brian Urquhart, *Hammarskjöld* (New York: Alfred A. Knopf, 1972), 458–469.

10. Henry Kissinger, *Diplomacy* (New York: Simon & Schuster, 1994), 443–444.

11. Alain Minc, *Le Syndrome Finlandais* (Paris: Editions du Seuil, 1986).

12. Henry Kissinger, *A World Restored: The Politics of Conservatism in a Revolutionary Age* (New York: Grosset & Dunlap, 1964), 20–21.

13. Tony Judt, *A Grand Illusion?* (New York: Hill and Wang, 1996), 26.

## Chapter 4

1. Helmut Schmidt, *Die Deutschen und Ihre Nachbarn* (Berlin: Siedler Verlag, 1990), 394–395.

2. Lennart Meri's interview as above (see note 7, chapter 2).

3. *International Herald Tribune*, December 13, 1988.

4. Jack Matlock, Jr., *Autopsy of an Empire* (New York: Random House, 1995), 245–246.

5. Liah Greenfeld, *Nationalism: Five Roads to Modernity* (Cambridge: Harvard University Press, 1992), 473.

6. Reported in the Finnish newspaper *Helsingin Sanomat*, April 16, 1997.

7. Youssef M. Ibrahim, "Finland Is Zooming into Cyberspace," *International Herald Tribune*, March 3, 1997.

8. François Duchêne, *Jean Monnet: The First Statesman of Interdependence* (New York: W. W. Norton & Company, 1994), 387.

## Chapter 5

1. Kissinger, *Diplomacy*, 824.

2. International Commission to Inquire into the Causes and Conduct of the Balkan Wars, *The Other Balkan Wars: A 1913 Carnegie Endowment Inquiry in Retrospect*, with a new introduction and reflections on the present conflict by George F. Kennan (Washington, D.C.: Carnegie Endowment for International Peace, 1993). See Kennan's introduction, "The Balkan Crisis: 1913 and 1993."

3. A.J.P. Taylor, *Bismarck: The Man and the Statesman* (London: Random House, Arrow Books, 1961), 167.

4. *International Herald Tribune*, October 20, 1994.

5. Taylor, *Bismarck*, 167.

6. Edward N. Luttwak, "Where Are the Great Powers? At Home with the Kids," *Foreign Affairs* 73 (July/August 1994): 23–28.

7. Quoted by Henry Kissinger in *Diplomacy*, 417.

8. *International Herald Tribune*, January 13, 1994.

9. Quoted in *Time* magazine, Golden Anniversary Issue, Winter 1996.

10. Quoted by Martin Walker in his article entitled "Present at the Solution," *World Policy Journal*, Spring 1997.

11. Ibid.

12. Foreign Minister de Charette's speech before the Institut des Hautes Etudes de la Defense Nationale, April 2, 1996.

13. *Newsweek*, February 13, 1997.

14. Speech by Strobe Talbott at Stanford University, September 19, 1997.

15. Mikhail Gorbachev, *Erinnerungen* (Berlin: Siedler Verlag, 1995), 1010–1027.

16. *European Security and Finnish Defence*, Report by the Council of State to Parliament, March 17, 1997.

## Chapter 6

1. Richard Pipes, *A Concise History of the Russian Revolution* (New York: Vintage Books, 1996), 396.

2. Quoted in *Helsingin Sanomat*, October 18, 1997.

3. Quoted by Sherman Garnett, "Russia's Illusory Ambitions," *Foreign Affairs* (March/April 1997).

4. Speech by Strobe Talbott at Stanford University on September 19, 1997.


## Conclusion

1. Reported in *Helsingin Sanomat*, May 16, 1997.

2. Organization for Economic Cooperation and Development, *Technology and Industrial Performance*, 1996.

3. *International Herald Tribune*, May 5, 1997.

4. *Politique Etrangère*, June 1980, p. 463.

5. *Time* magazine, July 7, 1997.

6. *Independent*, July 7, 1997.

# Selected Bibliography

Blomstedt, Yrjo, and Matti Klinge, eds. *J.K. Paasikiven Paivakirjat 1944–1956* [The diaries of J.K. Paasikivi 1944–1956]. 2 vols. Helsinki: WSOY, 1985–1986.

Bullock, Alan. *Ernest Bevin, Foreign Secretary, 1945–1951.* New York, London: W.W. Norton & Company, 1983.

Deutscher, Isaac. *Stalin: A Political Biography.* London: Oxford University Press, 1949.

Engman, Max, and David Kirby, eds. *Finland: People, Nation, State.* London: C. Hurst & Co., 1989.

Hobsbawm, Eric. *The Age of Extreme: The Short Twentieth Century, 1914–1991.* London: Michael Joseph, 1994.

Jakobson, Max. *The Diplomacy of the Winter War.* Cambridge, Mass.: Harvard University Press, 1961.

————. *Finnish Neutrality.* London: Hugh Evelyn, 1968.

Judt, Tony. *A Grand Illusion?* New York: Hill and Wang, 1996.

Jutikkala, Eino, and Kauko Pirinen. *A History of Finland.* Porvoo, Finland: WSOY, 1996.

Kennan, George F. "The Balkan Crisis: 1913 and 1993." In *The Other Balkan Wars: A 1913 Carnegie Endowment Inquiry in Retrospect*, International Commission to Inquire into the Causes and Conduct of the Balkan Wars. Washington, D.C.: Carnegie Endowment for International Peace, 1993.

Killham, Edward L. *The Nordic Way.* Washington, D.C.: Compass Press, 1993.

Kissinger, Henry. *Diplomacy.* New York: Simon & Schuster, 1994.

Klinge, Matti. *A Brief History of Finland.* Helsinki: Otava, 1997.

Koivisto, Mauno. *Witness to History: Memoirs of Mauno Koivisto, President of Finland 1982–1994.* London: C. Hurst & Co., 1997.

Lappalainen, Matti. *C.G.E. Mannerheim: The Marshal of Finland.* Helsinki: Recallmed, 1989.

Mead, W.R. *An Experience of Finland.* London: C. Hurst & Co., 1993.

Polvinen, Tuomo. *Between East and West: Finland in International Politics, 1944–1947.* Minneapolis: University of Minnesota Press, 1986.

Ries, Tomas. *Cold Will: The Defence of Finland.* London: Brassey's Defence Publishers, 1988.

Snellman, J.W. *Näin Puhui Snellman* [Thus spoke Snellman]. Helsinki: WSOY, 1960.

Tiitta, Allan, ed. *Find Out about Finland.* Helsinki: Otava, 1996.

Tillotson, H.M. *Finland at Peace and War.* Wilby, Norwich: Michael Russell, 1996.

Urquhart, Brian. *Hammarskjöld.* New York: Alfred A. Knopf, 1972.

Volkogonov, Dmitri. *Stalin: Triumph and Tragedy.* London: Weidenfeld and Nicolson, 1991.

Zetterberg, Seppo. *Finland after 1917.* Helsinki: Otava, 1991.

# Index

Herder, Johann Gottfried von, 13–14
Hitler, Adolf, 35, 41, 45
Hobsbawm, Eric, 2
Honecker, Erich, 82
Hungary: as candidate for NATO membership, 136; EU proposal for membership for, 123; German investment in and aid to, 132; mutual assistance pact with Soviet Union, 57; Soviet tanks in (1956), 67; uprising (1956), 42
Hunter, Robert, 130, 144

Iklé, Fred, 37
Immigration policy, Finland and Sweden, 97
Industrial sector: in postwar Finland, 90–94, 157–159; Sweden, 97; value-added of forest industry, 113

Jarring, Gunnar, 77
Johnston, Donald, 159
Judt, Tony, 89

Kant, Immanuel, 122
Karelia: postwar resettlement of people from, 54, 90; Russia's opposition to returning, 105
Karelian Isthmus: Soviet attack on Finnish troops (1944), 38; Soviet focus on acquisition of, 31–32; Soviet offensive (1940), 34–35
Kekkonen, Urho, 22, 55, 59, 61; achievements during first term, 71–72; back-channel diplomacy of, 77–80, 86–87; biographical facts about, 68–69; election as president, 67; philosophy of, 68; position on Finnish neutrality, 64; position on nationalism, 22; relationship with Khrushchev, 71–72; relationship with Kosygin, 72; resignation and death (1981, 1986), 94, 99; strategy in dealing with Soviets, 71–73; treatment of Finnish Communist Party (1966), 77–80

Kennan, George: on approaching end of Communism, 79; on non-European characteristics in eastern Europe, 124–125; position on NATO enlargement, 135; on present Russian regime, 151–152
Kennedy, John F., 5, 71
Keynes, John Maynard, 122
Khrushchev, Nikita, 44–45, 65–68, 70–72, 92
Kissinger, Henry, 2, 77, 79, 85–86, 96, 120
Kohl, Helmut, 112
Koivisto, Mauno, 94, 103, 107, 111, 141
Kollontay, Alexandra, 44
Kosygin, Aleksei, 72
Kozyrev, Andrei, 135
Kundera, Milan, 4
Kuusinen, O. W., 33, 34, 44–45

Labor markets: effect of regulation in Europe, 114–115; four Nordic countries' common (1954), 93; unemployment, 114, 159
Labor unions, Finland, 115–116
Lake Ladoga, 32, 37
Lake Onega, 37
Land reforms, Finland, 23, 108
Lapland, 36, 39
Latvia: as candidate for NATO membership, 139; EU proposed membership for, 124, 139; seeks NATO and EU membership, 137
Lie, Tryggve, 75
Linkomies, Edwin, 55
Lipponen, Paavo, 113
Lithuania: as candidate for NATO membership, 139; EU proposed membership for, 124, 139; seeks NATO and EU membership, 137
Luttwak, Edward, 126

Maastricht Treaty (1991), 108, 112
Machiavelli, Niccolo, 73
Malraux, André, 40

# About the Author

Max Jakobson is a former diplomat who played a key role in the shaping of Finland's foreign policy during the Cold War. As Finnish ambassador to the United Nations, he was America's favorite candidate to succeed U Thant as secretary-general, but in 1971 he was vetoed by the Soviets, who preferred Kurt Waldheim. After leaving government service in 1975, Max Jakobson has written extensively on international affairs. His books include *The Diplomacy of the Winter War* (Harvard University Press), and *The United Nations in the 1990s—A Second Chance?* (Twentieth Century Fund). His columns are published frequently in the *International Herald Tribune*.

ISBN 0-275-96372-1

EAN

9 780275 963729

90000>

HARDCOVER BAR CODE